DATE DUE

A Guide to
San Antonio Architecture

Richard Payne

A GUIDE TO
San Antonio Architecture

THE SAN ANTONIO CHAPTER OF THE
AMERICAN INSTITUTE OF ARCHITECTS

EDITORS:
Chris Carson, AIA
William McDonald, AIA

CONSULTING EDITOR:
Larry Paul Fuller

EDITORIAL ASSISTANT:
Jeffrey Fetzer, AIA

WRITERS:
John Ferguson
Stephen Fox
Larry Paul Fuller
James Steely
Melanie Young

PHOTOGRAPHERS:
Michael Lyon
Melanie Rush
Tim Summa
Additional photo credits as noted

GRAPHIC DESIGNER:
Herman Dyal, AIA
Fuller/Dyal & Stamper

Designed by Herman Dyal
Printed in the United States of America

San Antonio Chapter, AIA
720 GPM Tower
San Antonio, Texas 78216

Library of Congress Cataloging in Publication Data

American Institute of Architects. San Antonio Chapter.
A Guide to San Antonio Architecture, Chris Carson, AIA, and William B. McDonald, AIA, ed.

Includes index.
1. Architecture—Texas—San Antonio—Guide books. 2. San Antonio (Tx.)—history—buildings—description. 3. San Antonio (Tx.)—architecture—guidebooks. I. Title II. Chris Carson, AIA, ed. III. William B. McDonald, AIA, ed. IV. Larry Paul Fuller, consulting ed.

Library of Congress Catalog Card Number: 86-61384

ISBN 0-9616842-0-8

Contents

Acknowledgments

We wish to extend special thanks to the Texas Masonry Institute, J. Gregg Borchelt, Executive Director; the San Antonio Masonry Institute, Robert W. Gibbon, Director; and the H.E.B. Company, Charles Butt, President, for their generous financial support.

We wish to recognize the San Antonio Conservation Society, with initial support by Mrs. Sherwood W. Inkley, President 1984-1985, and continuing support by Mrs. Sidney J. Francis II, President 1985-1986.

We also wish to thank the Associated General Contractors, San Antonio Chapter, Michael B. Gerescher, Executive Vice President and Robert Mitchell, President, for their support.

The front cover depicts a portion of the original drawing of *trompe l'oeil* architectural mural *Victory and Triumph* by Roland Rodriguez. The design, a telescoped multiple image of San Antonio architectural landmarks and classical symbols, won a statewide competition sponsored by Target Stores and the Business Committee for the Arts.

Editorial contributions of Stephen Fox were sponsored by the Anchorage Foundation of Houston.

San Antonio Chapter, American Institute of Architects Guidebook Committee:

Co-Chairmen:
Chris Carson, AIA
William McDonald, AIA

Committee Members:
Prentice Bradley, FAIA
Andrew Perez III, AIA
Ken Rehler, AIA
Stephen Souter, AIA
Bob Wise, AIA

Additional research and assistance was provided by the following individuals:

Larry Borins
Dianna Bravo
Herbert Denny
Craig Duncan
Katherine Gregor
David Harring
Gus Hinojosa
Gabriel Durand Hollis, AIA
Marianna Jones
Jim Keane
Jamie Lofgren
Jean McCormick
Louis Perez
Morgan Price, AIA
Wanda Smith
Stephen Stepan

Foreword

San Antonio has style. Some call it *charm*; some say it's *picturesque*; others say San Antonio has a certain *flavor*.

San Antonio's architectural style defies exact definition or categorization. It is not wholly one thing.

San Antonio architecture has the robust Baroque influence of the Spanish settlers, as the city was founded in 1718 by soldiers and priests sent to the new world by the King of Spain. Later came Anglo-Americans and the European immigrants— including the Germans and the French— each bringing with them memories of their own cultural heritage that surfaced as architectural influences. In the 1920s and '30s, San Antonio architecture was further enriched when an emerging modern city embraced soaring Gothic skyscrapers with echoes of Art-Deco designs.

As a response to climate and geography, our architecture often reflects the realities of summers that are hot and dry. Even in the age of air conditioning, many of our buildings respond to the real and psychological needs for shelter from the harsh sun through such devices as broad overhangs, thick walls, covered walks, and shaded courts. By comparison, winters are mild except when a norther blows through or a rare snow blankets the city. Spring and fall are the most delightful seasons, offering clear cloudless days with perfect Texas-blue skies.

San Antonio may still be best described by Sidney Lanier, as he wrote a century ago: "Like Mardi Gras on the austere brink of Lent. The gentle pace of life, the lilt of the Spanish tongue, sunburnt landscape foiled by lush, semi-tropical vegetation, proud public edifices, tree-lined residential streets, shady courtyards, secluded patios, time- and sometimes blood-stained walls, the remembering river—all these give San Antonio a romance and even charm that is missing in many American cities less prone to myths, more solidly entrenched in reality."

Somehow, this diversity of climate and culture has created a style of architecture that is much admired, much discussed, and uniquely Texas.

Chris Carson, AIA
William McDonald, AIA

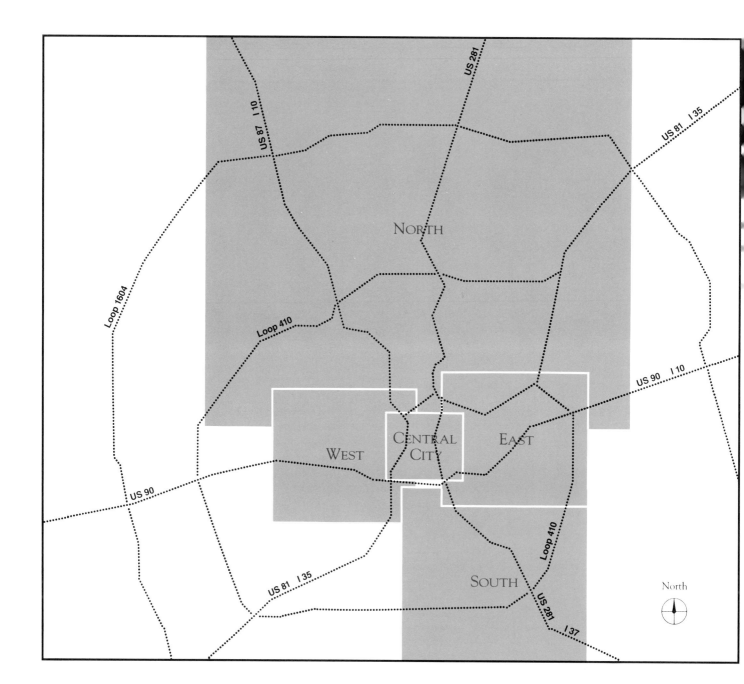

How to Use This Book

This guidebook is intended to provide the reader a tool for experiencing and appreciating the built environment of San Antonio as it has evolved over more than two and a half centuries. Following a general overview of the architectural development of the city, and an essay on the development of the River Walk, the guidebook treats 239 buildings, objects, and spaces as individual, consecutively numbered entries. The entries are organized by areas of the city—Central City, South, East, West, North, North-Central—and are keyed to a map of each area. The chronology of areas beginning with the Central City generally reflects that of the city's actual outward growth during its history. The listings are followed by brief profiles of nine architects who helped shape the face of the city, and an index to the individual entries.

Selections for this guidebook were made on the basis of architectural and/or historical merit. Each entry is accompanied by at least one photograph, a policy that had the effect of limiting the total number of entries page space would accommodate. The result is a selective, rather than comprehensive, presentation of San Antonio's architecture. The assortment presented here ultimately represents the opinions and judgment of the editors, the guidebook committee, and the writers, all of whom were dedicated to presenting a broad-based impression of the city.

Given the significance of peer recognition, all San Antonio buildings known to have been honored in a design award program sponsored by any component of the American Institute of Architects have been automatically included herein, except in certain instances wherein the current condition of the property precluded its being listed. AIA award-winning projects are designated by the following symbol placed beside the entry number: ★. Also included are historic sites listed in the National Register of Historic Places. National Register properties are designated by the initials NR.

As a general rule, sites are listed by their original, earliest-known, or most significant name. Site names do not necessarily reflect the current owner's name. Dates given represent the date of completion of a construction or development project and are followed by the site address and the name of the original architect or, in some cases, builder. Due to space limitations and considerations of emphasis, architects involved primarily with renovations have not always been noted.

Maps are intended to be schematic rather than literal, facilitating general location of each site listed, both within a given area and in the overall context of the city. Maps are therefore intended to be used in conjunction with a good street map. Listings within the dense Central City area are organized to facilitate touring by foot but are not presented as formal walking tours.

While the information contained herein has been processed with all due concern for accuracy, errors in a publication of this kind—one that relies on input from a broad range of sources—are inevitable. No legal responsibility is assumed by anyone associated with this publication regarding the competency or accuracy of any listings, or for the appreciation or depreciation in value of any premises by reason of their inclusion or exclusion. In the interest of possible subsequent editions, readers are invited to submit comments or corrections to the San Antonio Chapter of the American Institute of Architects.

Listing in this guidebook does not constitute the owner's or occupant's permission to trespass, invade privacy, or destroy property. For the most part, these guidebook sites can be viewed at least to some extent from public thoroughfares. Permission should be obtained before visiting any privately owned dwellings.

AN OVERVIEW
San Antonio and Its Architecture

Main Plaza San Antonio Texas.

Erhard Pentenrieder, "Main Plaza, San Antonio," c. 1859 detail from a songsheet by Marie Gentilz, (Daughters of the Republic of Texas Library at the Alamo). At the center is San Fernando Church, 1749, altered. Flanking it are a Creole-style house (right) and a German-style house (left).

In Texas the new is prized; in San Antonio the old persists. Texas is big and open; San Antonio's historic precincts are irregular and compact. Geographically and historically, San Antonio lies at the heart of Texas. Yet it has resisted assimilation into a pan-Texan identity.

At the root of this phenomenon lies the fact that San Antonio is a border town. Not in the sense of Brownsville, Laredo, or El Paso, those cities of the Rio Grande, although San Antonio shares with them the indelible imprint of Hispanic culture. But more like St. Louis, New Orleans, or San Francisco: a city that for much of its existence straddled a border between civilization and wilderness: a beacon of the former, a refuge from the latter; sustained by both, absorbed by neither. It is this legacy of wild frontier civilization that endows San Antonio's history with an epic dimension quite foreign to other large Texas cities.

And it is the city itself—its places and buildings—that most powerfully preserves and relays San Antonio's epic history, not as discrete incidents of pastness, but as documents of the continuity of human existence.

Architecture provides the most enduring and most visible memorials of San Antonio's existence, for, having been founded in 1718 by a group of Franciscan missionaries representing God and King, San Antonio is the third oldest surviving settlement in Texas and the only major city in the state whose existence predates 1836, the year Texas won its independence from Mexico. The five Spanish missions survive to reflect a primary motive for San Antonio's founding. The presidio captain's residence (known since its restoration in 1930 as the Spanish Governor's Palace) on the Plaza de Armas (now Military Plaza) bespeaks the practical method of securing isolated mission stations in 18th-century

Below: Herman Lungkwitz, "San Antonio de Bexar," c. 1857 (San Antonio Museum Association, San Antonio). A view westward along Crockett Street from Bonham Street. The
rear of the Alamo, which then housed the U.S. Army Quartermaster Depot, is at the right. Below right: Mission San Jose, (San Jose y San Miguel de Aguayo) 1768-70.

Spanish America. And the *parroquia* of Nuestra Senora de Candelaria y Guadalupe (now San Fernando Cathedral) on the Plaza de las Islas (now Main Plaza) commemorates the civil settlement of the villa of San Fernando de Bexar by the colony of transplanted Canary Islanders in 1731.

As might be expected, central San Antonio is a virtual architectural and urban palimpsest. Parts of it—Military and Main plazas, La Villita, and Milam Square—comprised the old Creole villa and its suburbs. This was the San Antonio that was the capital of the *provincia* of Texas during the last half century of the Spanish viceregal era. This also was the San Antonio of the period of Mexican ascendency, and it was the vulnerable frontier city of the short-lived Republic of Texas.

Present-day Alamo Plaza; the retail and entertainment district along Houston Street and around Travis Park; the zones north, east, and south of Alamo Plaza; and the rehabilitated residential district along King William Street comprised the new neighborhoods of a San Antonio resuscitated by the annexation of Texas to the United States in 1846. When, as the one inland city in Texas, it began to attract settlers and traders—not only Anglo Americans, but French and German colonists, who had commenced settlement in central Texas in the middle 1840s—this rude, violent, isolated outpost acquired an unexpected cosmopolitan tone. Frederick Law Olmsted commented on this attribute when he visited San Antonio in the middle 1850s, noting especially the variety of building types that this diversity entailed. Although Olmsted did not identify specific architects and builders, it was in San Antonio that the nas-

cent profession of architecture was most firmly rooted in Texas, represented by two Franco-Americans, Francois P. Giraud and his brother T.E. Giraud, and the Germans John Fries, W.C.A. Thielpape, David Russi, and John H. Kampmann. Fries was the superior talent, as his Casino Hall (1858, demolished), Menger Hotel (1859, greatly altered), City Market House (1858, demolished), and First Presbyterian Church (1860, demolished) demonstrated. Ironically, his best-known surviving work could be one for which he has received insufficient credit. According to some historians, Fries in 1850 repaired the shattered ruin of the Alamo church; it was he who is thought to have given it the distinctive shaped parapet that has become its emblem.

The San Antonio of the southwest frontier, portrayed in the paintings of Hermann

Theodore Gentilz, "El convite para el baile,"
(Daughters of the Republic of Texas Library at
the Alamo, Gentilz Collection). Gentilz's
genre paintings depict daily life in Creole San
Antonio.

Below left: J. Riely Gordon, Project: Kampmann Estate Building, c. 1893 (The American Architect and Building News, vol. 42, January 20, 1894, plate section).

Below right: John Fries and David Russi, City Market House, 1859, demolished 1925 (Daughters of the Republic of Texas Library at the Alamo).

Lungkwitz and Theodore Gentilz and in the descriptive accounts of Sidney Lanier and O. Henry, began to be transformed after the Civil War, especially after 1877 when the arrival of railroad connections brought an end to its isolation. With a trade territory that extended from the Gulf of Mexico through south and central Texas and well into northern Mexico, San Antonio grew rapidly during the last quarter of the 19th century. It was then that the King William area—an elite suburban neighborhood where wealthy Germans constructed a number of large houses— came into its own, as did Goliad Street in the Barrio del Alamo (now HemisFair Plaza). Wealthy Anglo-Americans lived near Travis Park and along Broadway and Alamo Street,

north of Alamo Plaza, as well as in new areas, such as Nolan Street, to the east of Alamo Plaza. These were neighborhoods that all but vanished after the 1940s and '50s.

Between the middle 1870s and the middle 1880s, the first generation of architects gave way to a host of newcomers: the Englishman Alfred Giles; the Irishman James Murphy; two young native Texans, Albert F. Beckmann and James Wahrenberger (both of whom were trained in Germany); and the *wunderkind* of 19th-century Texas architecture, James Riely Gordon. These architects introduced to the main streets and plazas of San Antonio, as well as the new suburbs, tall, bulky, aggressively massed and decorated examples of Amer-

ican High Victorian architecture, overbearing the antebellum and Creole building stock.

James Riely Gordon was the preeminent architect of late 19th-century San Antonio. He brought to his work a high level of formal development, orchestrating composition, proportion, constructive and ornamental details, and spatial sensation with a sophistication that was unmatched locally.

San Antonio, in the late 19th century, was affected by another architectural phenomenon that was to exert, if slowly at first, considerable impact. This was the notion that the city possessed a distinct tradition of architecture, one that might continue to inform new building. The local color movement in American literature

Above: J. Flood Walker, St. Anthony Hotel,
1910 (The Southern Architectural Review,
December, 1910, Houston Public Library,
Metropolitan Research Center). Right: Atlee
B. & Robert M. Ayres, Martin Wright Electric
Company Building, 1929 (Atlee B. & Robert
M. Ayres Collection, The Architectural Draw-
ings Collection, Architecture and Planning
Library, The University of Texas at Austin).

Herbert S. Green, San Antonio Express News *Building, 1929* (San Antonio Express News).

stimulated a fascination with regional subcultures that San Antonio, with its "exotic" mix of cultures, proved well able to engage. The New York architect Cyrus L.W. Eidlitz apparently was the first to perceive the existence of a locally colorful architectural tradition, and he used this perception as a point of departure for his design of the San Antonio National Bank Building (1886). Its Mooresque detail paid homage to the curious Mudejar arched portal of the church at San Francisco de la Espada.

Not until the turn of the century, though, did this local architectural tradition surface in large-scale projects. It was a San Francisco architect, D.J. Patterson, who used the Alamo church as a source of inspiration for the Southern Pacific Passenger Station (1902), followed by Harvey L. Page's International & Great Northern Railway Passen-

ger Station (1906), J. Flood Walker's Mission-style St. Anthony Hotel (1909 and 1910, altered), and the church-like Missouri, Kansas & Texas Railway Passenger Station (1917, demolished), by Frederick Sterner of New York.

After the turn of the century the established Victorian architects (minus Gordon, who moved his practice to New York in 1902) were joined by a younger contingent of professionals. Some, like Harvey L. Page, Carl V. Seutter, or George Willis, were recent arrivals. But a suprising number (by Texas standards) were men who had grown up in San Antonio, most notably Atlee B. Ayres, Leo M.J. Dielmann, Henry T. Phelps, and Carleton W. Adams.

The city's physical expansion, made practicable in the 1890s with the electrification of the streetcar lines, became widespread in

the early 1900s. The virtual rebuilding of large sectors of the downtown area (especially along Houston Street, which challenged Commerce Street's primacy as the main street of downtown San Antonio) was precipitated by a massive program of street realignment, street widening, and bridge construction. Skyscrapers began to dot the horizon, many produced by two out-of-town architectural firms, Mauren, Russell & Garden of St. Louis (Mauren, Russell & Crowell after 1912) and Sanguinet & Staats of Fort Worth. Suburban development followed a leap-frog pattern on all sides of downtown. To the north, along Main Avenue, a series of restricted private-place neighborhoods (known collectively as Laurel Heights) began to be developed in the 1890s, simultaneous with the first garden suburb in Texas, Alamo Heights (1890).

San Antonio reached its apogee during the first quarter of the 20th century. The rise of a Mediterranean architectural genre, based upon the "minor" architecture of Spain, freely adapted to contemporary building types and programs, was the most visible and arresting fact of local architecture during the 1920s and 1930s. Like the earlier Mission style, the Mediterranean had its origin in California. But its implicit connotation of Hispanic tradition made it irresistible in San Antonio, where it might plausibly be represented as an indigenous vernacular.

Yet it was not stylistic uniformity that made the architecture of this period so compelling, but a tacit architectural agreement, an unformulated set of conventions, that— at least in historical perspective—produced an unobsessive consistency. These conven-

tions imbued San Antonio architecture of the 1920s with an urbanity and sense of local particularity that transcends style. A penchant for rich ornamental detail, affirmation of the primacy of the street facade, a deftness at turning street corners, and a preference for brown tapestry brick were recurring architectural characteristics.

Against the background of modern transformations that engulfed San Antonio during the 1920s, the growth of an urban conservation movement figures strongly. The acquisition of the Alamo *convento* site in 1905 by the Daughters of the Republic of Texas and the organization of the San Antonio Conservation Society in 1924 (by 15 women intent on preserving not only local historical landmarks but the environmental characteristics that made San Antonio special) were the two pivotal events. These led from a merely nostalgic extolling of the "charm" of old San Antonio to a program of action to ensure protection of the city's heritage and character.

The stage thus was set for two significant acts of urban reclamation that occurred in the late 1930s under the sponsorship of Mayor Maury Maverick: construction of the River Walk according to the plans of Robert H.H. Hugman (1941), and the restoration of three blocks of small mid-19th-century houses in La Villita as a craft center, carried out by a young Dallas architect, O'Neil Ford.

Ford's selection for this job was providential, for in the late 1940s he and Milton Ryan resuscitated the moribund architectural scene in San Antonio with their spirited displays of Modern architectural production. Both were especially concerned with structural clarity, material economy, openness, and simplicity. Ryan adopted the steel lally column and the laminated wood beam as the constructional essentials of his lithe, elegant Modern style. Ford worked in reinforced concrete, becoming the first San Antonio architect to articulate concrete construction architecturally, despite its long history of use locally. During the 1950s, younger architects were inspired by

Jesse C. Trevino, "Los santos de San Antonio," 1980 (Texas Images and Visions, Austin: Archer M. Huntington Art Gallery, 1983, P. 161).

the examples of Ryan and Ford to design unpretentious, economical, conscientiously detailed Modern buildings that paid special attention to site and climatic conditions.

Ford's adherence to a Regionalist attitude informed his approach to Modernism. For though he shared the aversion to historical eclecticism typical of the 1950s, he did not reject the architecture of the past. In San Antonio, it was Modern architects (along with some of the older eclectic generation, especially Harvey P. Smith and Marvin Eickenroht) who advocated historic preservation and rehabilitation of the older central city neighborhoods, such as the King William area, where O'Neil Ford moved his office in 1954. And they advocated infill buildings that sought to reconcile Modernism with an acknowledgment of local vernacular, particularly in the use of the segmental arch.

Unfortunately, during the 1960s, a far less respectful and intelligent approach to urban renewal was pursued, resulting in the devastation of near-town residential neighborhoods to the east, south, and west of downtown, the razing of many architecturally-historically important buildings, and the displacement of many lower-income residents. HemisFair '68, a world's fair exposition produced to celebrate the 250th anniversary of the founding of San Antonio, exemplified both the best and worst approaches. The large houses along Goliad Street were saved, but most of the rest of the Barrio del Alamo was obliterated, despite an appeal by O'Neil Ford, the fair's initial consulting architect, that the neighborhood be adapted to contain the fair.

Beginning in the late 1970s, San Antonio experienced an urban reawakening. One indication was a construction boom of a magnitude not experienced since the 1920s. Much of the new building that resulted was dispersed along the northern rim of freeways in speculative office towers. Throughout central San Antonio, older buildings were carefully rehabilitated. Unfortunately, however, the decline of the downtown retail district was not arrested. Whether tall office building construction and intensive development of tourist attractions can provide a satisfactory substitute for traditional downtown amenities remains problematic. City-sponsored urban renewal has been redirected to neighborhood conservation and economic development, as demonstrated by St. Paul Square, Avenida Guadalupe, and Cattleman's Square.

San Antonio architecture also experienced an amazing renascence beginning in the late 1970s, wherein the city's Baroque and vernacular traditions have been fused in an intense, exuberant new school of local architecture, one that sums up in uninhibited ways the qualities peculiar to its place. San Antonio is a captivating city, largely because so many of its citizens value the city as a place—not just as an investment opportunity—and seem willing to learn the lessons it has to teach. New San Antonio architecture exhibits a keen awareness to lessons from the past—both ancient and modern—in order to continue building a city that is rich in provocative architecture and inviting public places.

A HISTORY
The River Walk

The Indians named it *Yanaguana* for "refreshing waters." And throughout the vast land called *Tejas*, Spanish colonists viewed the meandering San Antonio River and its lush valley as an oasis, a rest haven for weary expeditions crisscrossing the territory. Eventually, each of the San Antonio missions was established near the river to draw from its nurturing waters and fertile floodplain. From the very beginning, San Antonio has been defined and sustained by its river.

If the river is the life force—the main artery—of San Antonio, the Paseo del Rio is the very heart of the city. Better known as the River Walk, this 1.8-mile horseshoe-shaped bend in the river lingers in popular consciousness as part of the definitive image of San Antonio—the essence of its myth, the focus of its identity.

The River Walk is one of those rare amenities on whose merits architects, urban planners, and everyday people agree. One reliable measure of its success is that tourists and natives alike find its charms irresistible. Following the winding course of the river on either side, some 15 feet below street level, the walk is lined with outdoor cafes, shops, galleries, bars, and hotels—all in a lush green setting animated by the movement of water and the constant flow of people. Tall cypress trees and dense banks of exotic plants and foliage constitute a year-round botanical garden—removed from the heat and pollution of the street—into which a thriving cosmopolitan subculture has been inserted.

A stroll through the Paseo is a rich visual and tactile experience: ever-shifting vistas; views framed by graceful street and pedestrian bridges; continually changing patterns of old stone masonry on high curving walls and on the walk underfoot; splotches of sun and shade by day, colorful lights by night. The River Walk is its own microcosm, yet it is one with the city, whose hovering presence and accessibility are manifested through occasional glimpses from below. Rather than creating a schism within the dense city center, the Paseo ties it together.

Cited as a distinguished achievement in the 1984 honors program of the American Institute of Architects, the River Walk was praised as "a masterpiece of urban design that demonstrated to the world how a modest natural feature can be made the focus of public activity and affection." But the river bend has not always been held in such high esteem; indeed, at one point in its history it came dangerously close to being paved over as a storm sewer.

By the early 1900s, the downtown river had become more of a liability than an asset—an unsightly polluted stream lined with rubbish, vagrants, and the neglected backsides of commercial buildings. Rather than a pedestrian amenity, the river bend was a veritable alley. Furthermore, it posed a dangerous threat from flooding. Many small floods and two fairly serious ones in 1913 resulted in a 1919 study that proposed, among other measures, the paving over of numerous bends in the river, including the horseshoe bend that is now the River Walk. The study predicted disastrous loss of life and property if such measures were not implemented.

Unfortunately, these predictions came true in 1921 when a raging flood put downtown streets under nine feet of water, left 50 people dead in its wake, and caused $50 million in property damage. There was an immediate outcry to implement the previously proposed flood prevention plan. But there were also a number of farsighted, outspoken, and influential citizens who sensed the ultimate potential of the river, and who bitterly opposed the suggestion that it become a paved boulevard with sewer pipes beneath it.

As city officials contemplated the proposal, a group of concerned citizens intent on saving the river banded together as the San Antonio Conservation Society, now a model for preservation and conservation groups across the country. As part of the Society's campaign, its president—an artist known affectionately as "Miss Emily" Edwards—wrote and produced a puppet show entitled "The Goose that Laid the Golden Egg," which illustrated the folly of obliterating one of the city's greatest assets. The Society was successful in gaining a reprieve for the river bend, but the controversy continued for the rest of the decade. Still remaining was the consummate vision of what the river could become.

That vision began to emerge in 1927 when architect Robert H.H. Hugman returned to San Antonio from New Orleans, where he had been deeply impressed by that city's charm as reflected in the restoration of the French Quarter. Inspired by memories of New Orleans, as well as the quaint, winding streets of "Old Spain," Hugman imagined transforming the river bend area into a place that would reflect San Antonio's Spanish, Mexican and Southwestern heritage. In 1929, Hugman began talking to city officials, citizens groups, and anyone who would listen about the components of his vision: "a quaint, old cobblestoned street rambling lazily along

the river. A street with old world appeal. Small shops, a studio apartment . . . , a cafe, cabaret and dance club. . . ." He spoke of "gaily colored boats fashioned after the gondolas of Venice" and a "boat ride down the river on a balmy night, fanned by a gentle breeze carrying the delightful aroma of honeysuckle and sweet olive, old-fashioned street lamps casting fantastic shadows on the surface of the water, strains of soft music in the air. . . ."

Hugman's words were delicious and captivating, but perhaps even more effective at capturing the popular imagination was his elaborate set of drawings, maps, and watercolors. From these powerful images, citizens were able to grasp his romantic vision and make it their own. Hugman's scheme was all the more irresistible because, in addition to all its romantic imagery, it included a

simple but brilliant solution to the practical problem of flooding. He suggested bypassing the river bend with a channel, controlled by flood gates, linking the two tips of the U.

Although public and official support for Hugman's plan was strong, the Depression-Era timing was bad. But in 1938, with the help of San Antonio's U.S. Congressman Maury Maverick—a friend of Franklin Roosevelt—the city secured federal assistance through the Works Progress Administration and Hugman became the official architect of the River Beautification Project. Receiving national attention as the "Venice of America," the WPA project resulted in the construction of 17,000 feet of walkways, 31 stairways leading from 21 bridges, and the Arneson River Theater, as well as the planting of more than 11,000 trees and shrubs. Mature cypress trees were

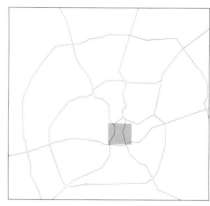

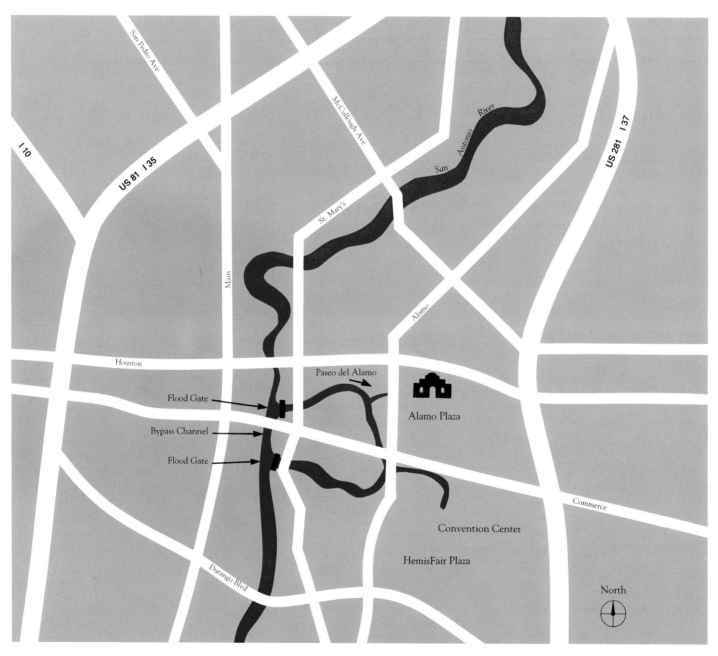

San Pedro Ave

McCullough Ave

San Antonio River

San

I 10

US 81 I 35

US 281 I 37

St. Mary's

Main

Alamo

Houston

Paseo del Alamo

Alamo Plaza

Flood Gate

Bypass Channel

Flood Gate

Commerce

Convention Center

HemisFair Plaza

Durango Blvd

North

carefully preserved, and others were transplanted from the nearby Guadalupe River.

By 1941, the essence of Hugman's dream
had come true. But with the distractions of
World War II and the subsequent flight to
the suburbs came another era of neglect for
the river. By the late '50s people were talking about its unrealized potential, and in
1962 the River Walk Advisory Commission
was created to help guide its development as
a commercial and entertainment area. The
proposed HemisFair '68 celebration of the
city's 250th birthday further increased
momentum, and the San Antonio Chapter
of AIA was asked to produce a plan for the
river's revitalization.

An 11-member AIA committee headed
by Cyrus Wagner produced a comprehensive plan that called for linking major nodes
and spaces at street level as well as new
development and capital improvements
along the river itself. In the same way that
Hugman's drawings were persuasive in com-
municating his vision, the committee's
sketches were inspirational, conveying a
clear sense of how buildings might be made
to relate to the river in the interest of
renewed vitality. In 1964, the city passed a
$30 million bond issue to implement many
of the ideas in the plan and, in anticipation
of HemisFair, extended the river to the
Convention Center. Also added were new
lighting and new entrances to the River
Walk, a marina for party barges, river taxis,
and pedalboats.

Since that time, an ever-increasing
number of establishments have contributed
to the vitality of the downtown river network. Gone forever are the days when the
economic potential of the river went
unrealized. The new and continuing chal-

lenge is to monitor development so as to
protect the unique qualities of the River
Walk that form the substance of its appeal.
The current issues being addressed by concerned professionals and citizens groups
relate not to catalysts for development, but
problems associated with it. There is much
concern, for example, that while high land
costs dictate vertical development along
the river, the net effect of too many tall
buildings would be "canyonization" and the
attendant loss of sky and sunlight to buildings and shadow. Gone would be the
almost-magical quality of light gently
filtered through cypress trees, as well as
many species of exotic plants that could not
survive without it.

In addition to new policies affecting the
River Walk per se, the city faces decisions
regarding the whole 10-mile river corridor
and its development from the core of the
city south to the missions, and north to the
headwaters in Brackenridge Park. Being
sought now is a new and more comprehensive vision—a plan that will carry the life
force of San Antonio into the 21st century
with all the grace and appeal a peaceful little
river should have.

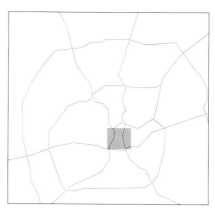

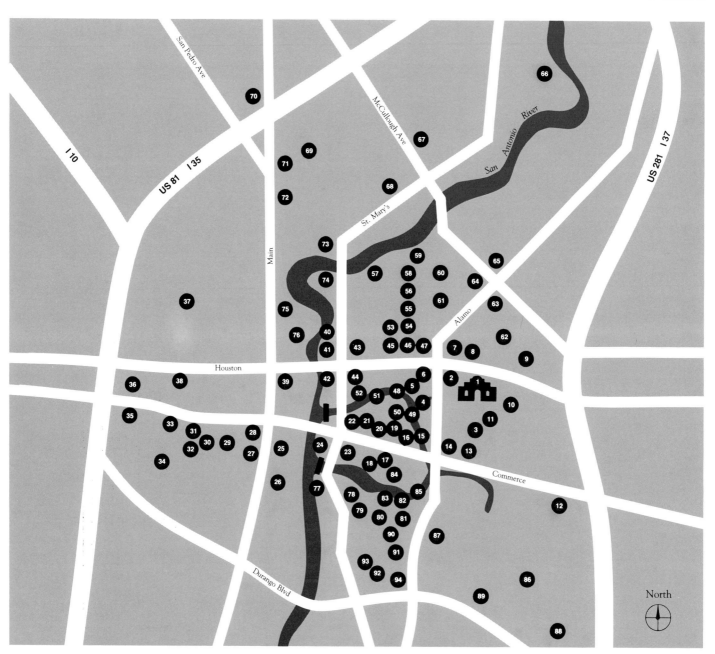

North

Central City

Although the core of San Antonio retains few visible architectural reminders of the city's 18th-century heritage, the layout of the streets and public spaces still corresponds to the earliest known map of the city, drafted by Jose de Urrutia in 1767. The slight irregularities in the city's street grid no doubt reflect the conditions of life in Colonial San Antonio, when platting necessarily took second place to the rigors of defending the populace against hostile acts of the Comanche and Apache tribes.

The city's dual public squares, one dominated by San Fernando Cathedral and the other by City Hall, constitute something of an anomaly, since traditional Spanish Colonial town planning gave the dual authorities of church and state equal prominence on a single square.

San Antonio's growth was limited to the central-city area until after Texas won its independence from Mexico in 1836. Even with the tremendous growth that took place in the second half of the 19th century, great respect was paid to the early plan of the city and to the symbolic nature of Main and Military Plazas. The massive Bexar County Courthouse and the slightly eccentric City Hall were logically placed at the heart of the 18th-century plan, further consolidating governmental authority on the plazas. Alamo Plaza became a major site of commercial development, while Commerce Street became the prime location for the city's banking and financial institutions.

The onset of the 20th century brought major architectural changes to the central-city area, as modest skyscrapers began to join the ornate commercial buildings of local architects such as J. Riely Gordon and James Wahrenberger. Some of the city's more prominent designs were sited with no apparent logic or sense of tradition; Ralph Cameron's monumental Medical Arts Building, for example, was situated just opposite the revered Alamo. The city's building boom came to a halt with the Great Depression, but not before the city acquired a new architectural symbol in the Smith-Young Tower of 1929.

It took the city's great urban gesture, the Paseo del Rio, to knit together all of downtown San Antonio, artfully combining flood control with commerce and pedestrian space. While the central city has yet to fill in the void left by HemisFair in 1968, it remains the vital heart of San Antonio for native and visitor alike.

1 NR
THE ALAMO, 1744
(Mission San Antonio de Valero)
Alamo Plaza
Antonio Tello and Hieronimo Ybarra,
    master masons
Rebuilt with parapet, 1850
Credited to John Fries

Once part of a large mission complex established in 1724, the present Alamo church was begun in 1744. Its facade was intended to reflect a common Spanish configuration with twin bell towers, but these evidently were never finished. Heavy limestone walls made the church and its adjacent compound an ideal fortress, and the Alamo was subsequently garrisoned by Spanish and Mexican troops. Settlers in the Mexican state of Texas rebelled in 1835 and seized the Alamo, making a heroic but fatal stand here in early 1836. When Texan independence was won, little remained of the complex besides a few heavy walls and the delicate stone carving of the church's frontispiece.

Nevertheless, the U.S. Army repaired the church and other buildings after Texas joined the Union in 1845. The Quartermaster Corps built the now-familiar parapet over the unfinished facade in 1850, with a profile designed to disguise the church's new gabled roof. By 1882 the church had become a symbol of the battle a half century before, and the state purchased the shrine. Alfred Giles's son E. Palmer Giles designed a reinforced-concrete vaulted roof for the structure in 1920, similar to the intended original design.

2 NR
ALAMO PLAZA, from circa 1724

Much of the present Alamo Plaza was formerly the mission's enclosed courtyard.
Recent digs have located the ancient wall
perimeters; the original outlines are
reflected in paving stones laid in front of the
Alamo church and in excavated wall foundations on the west side. After the 1836
Texan defeat here, the Mexican army
demolished much of the enclosed compound, but the U.S. Army cleared the area
and occupied the remaining stone buildings
after 1847. The Quartermaster Depot in the
Alamo church attracted trading houses and
hotels, and by 1850 the open plaza was the
busiest site in the city. Although the Army
moved out of the Alamo in 1878, the location of the post office at the plaza's north
end in 1887 and the Joske Brothers store at
the south in 1888 established the plaza as a
lively urban space, and the city assumed
landscaping responsibilities.

3 NR
MENGER HOTEL, 1859
204 Alamo Plaza
John Fries
South addition, 1909
Alfred Giles

The Menger's north wing was originally a
subtle Greek Revival edifice built to serve
the noisy commercial district growing up
around the Army's Quartermaster Depot in
the Alamo. By 1909 the Alamo was prop-
erly regarded as a shrine and the city had
converted the busy market area to a park-
like plaza. Giles' addition reflected the city's
growing sophistication with an exuberance
of Renaissance Revival details, executed in
stuccoed brick, cast iron, and pressed metal.
An interior rotunda provided light and a
circulation hub, each level marked with
Corinthian columns and filigreed
balustrades.

4 NR
REUTER BUILDING, 1891
217 Alamo Plaza
James Wahrenberger

Although not quite as dramatic or inventive
as Wahrenberger's superb San Antonio
Turnverein of the same year, the William
Reuter Building is nevertheless one of the
best late 19th-century commercial buildings
in the city. Of special note are the two projecting bays on the second floor, which must
provide outstanding views of the Alamo
across the street. With so important a
neighbor, one can presume that the architect, either on his own or at the prompting
of his client, considered such luxuries a
worthwhile expense. For many years this
building was draped in an applied metal skin
that, fortunately, has been removed.

Rick Gardner

5 ★
PASEO DEL ALAMO, 1981
300 Block, Alamo Plaza
Ford, Powell & Carson

This public pedestrian concourse connects Alamo Plaza with the River Walk, two blocks to the west. At the Alamo Plaza entrance are fragments of the west wall of Mission San Antonio de Valero's patio. In its progress from these archeological remains to the river, the paseo steps down repeatedly, conveying pedestrians alongside—and beneath—channeled waters that course insistently downward to the river, 27 feet below the level of Alamo Plaza. The paseo even penetrates the 16-story lobby of the Hyatt Regency Hotel before reaching its destination beneath the Presa Street bridge.

6 NR
CROCKETT BLOCK, 1882-83
317-323 Alamo Plaza
Alfred Giles
Rehabilitated, 1984-85
Humberto Saldana and Associates

This ensemble of four three-story buildings with a common Italianate facade was built along the old west wall of the Alamo's courtyard for entrepreneurs William and Albert Maverick. Giles articulated the design with cast-iron piers on the ground level, angular and round arches of limestone above, capped with an entablature of pressed metal. By the early 1980s, various false fronts and awkward window blinds obscured the original harmony shared by the four buildings. While the Paseo del Alamo was being constructed as a pedestrian connection between the river and Alamo Plaza, the Crockett Block was rediscovered and its facade restored.

7 NR
UNITED STATES POST OFFICE AND COURTHOUSE, 1937
615 East Houston Street
Ralph H. Cameron
Paul Philippe Cret, consulting architect

The vast, five-story, limestone-faced Post Office (which supplanted its castellated Romanesque predecessor of 1891) is an exemplary work of monumental urban architecture. The French-born Philadelphia architect, Paul Philippe Cret, who during the 1930s executed major architectural commissions in Texas—all in a single, full-bodied classical style—deployed the beautifully modulated elevations of the Post Office to wall up the north end of Alamo Plaza and create a sense of bounded open space. Yet he did so without making the Post Office compete for attention with the Alamo itself. The restrained classical detailing rewards careful study; the vestibule just inside the main entrance contains Howard Cook's fresco mural *San Antonio's Importance in Texas History* of 1939.

8 NR
MEDICAL ARTS BUILDING, 1926
705 East Houston Street
Ralph H. Cameron

Cameron clad this V-plan structure with cut stone on the first two floors; the upper 11 floors were encrusted with Gothic details in terra cotta, topped with a flying-buttressed corner turret and a Chateauesque mansard roof. Once housing doctors' offices and a hospital, the building has been tastefully converted as the Emily Morgan Hotel.

9
TURNVEREIN, 1891
411 Bonham Street
James Wahrenberger

Located in an area that has suffered greatly from demolition, the Turnverein stands as a testament to the significance of the Society of Turners in 19th-century San Antonio. As the leading social and cultural organization of the city's German community, the Turners surely demanded and got a design that would proclaim their status in the city. Wahrenberger, the son of Swiss-immigrant parents, here produced his most sophisticated work, an enlarged version of the Reuter Building, which was rising on Alamo Plaza at the same time. The complexity of the main facade is almost overworked, but the building is nevertheless an excellent example of how Renaissance architectural elements were used before the architectural climate of the country changed with the World's Columbian Exposition of 1893. This structure would actually be more at home on the streets of Paris than in any American city of the period.

10 NR
CROCKETT HOTEL, 1901
301 East Crockett Street
Padgett (first name unknown)
Remodeled, 1983
Ford, Powell & Carson

The transformation of the Crockett Hotel from a nondescript building to one of the city's most noted hotels reflects a new fashion in adapting old structures to new tastes. While situated on an important site, just behind the Alamo, the Crockett was never the equal of the St. Anthony or the Gunter. The conversion of the hotel's light well into a glazed-in atrium provides for some dramatic moments on the interior, although the height of the resulting space is in conflict with the otherwise domestic character of the hotel. The small bar overlooking the Lady Bird Johnson Fountain is the most convivial space in the new creation, and the rooftop hot tub provides one of the most unusual means of viewing the Alamo, especially at night.

11
LADY BIRD JOHNSON FOUNTAIN, 1974
Intersection of Bonham and Crockett
Ford, Powell & Carson

One could be forgiven for assuming that this fountain has been here for decades, for the stone used in its construction and its relationship to its site successfully create that impression. Modeled on the generally more ornate public fountains of Mexico, the Johnson Fountain's subdued presence is perhaps fitting for its site just to the rear of the Alamo. Unfortunately, pedestrian enjoyment of the fountain is hampered by the constant presence of automobiles converging on the intersection.

12 NR
SCHROEDER-YTURRI HOUSE, Circa 1870
(City Water Board Museum)
1040 East Commerce Street

The earliest known owner of this one-story stuccoed-limestone house was George Schroeder, who lived here until 1910. Italianate details add a sophisticated note to an otherwise vernacular, symmetrical-plan residence, a good example of a typical late-19th-century San Antonio house. E.H. Yturri owned the house from 1936 to 1965.

13 NR
ST. JOSEPH'S CATHOLIC CHURCH,
1876
623 East Commerce Street
Theodore E. Giraud
Restored, 1981
Ford, Powell & Carson

The growing German-Catholic community
of the mid-19th-century in San Antonio
had worshipped with the Hispanic congre-
gations but, after the Civil War, expressed
a desire for a church of its own. A request
for the Alamo mission church was denied
(as the U.S. Army was using it for a supply
warehouse), so this Gothic Revival edifice
was begun nearby in 1868. Its limestone
walls were highlighted in 1898 by Wahrenberger's spire, and by art-glass windows
around the turn of the century.

14 NR
JOSKE'S DEPARTMENT STORE,
1939 and 1952
100 Alamo Plaza
Bartlett Cocke
John Graham Company, consulting
    architects

Cocke's massive five-story building for San
Antonio's oldest department store incorporates several earlier structures: Alfred Giles
& Guindon's original Joske Brothers store
of 1889 at the corner of Alamo Plaza and
Commerce, plus the extensive additions
that Leo M.J. Dielmann made to it in 1910.
All of these have been submerged beneath
a smooth limestone face that combines
Modernistic massing and composition with
florid Spanish Renaissance ornament. The
ground-floor shadow boxes, wreathed in

miniature reproductions of Mission San
Jose's famous sacristy window, never fail to
amuse—or shock. In successive additions
to Joske's, Cocke maintained the character
of his original design.

Rick Gardner

Rick Gardner

15
CLIFFORD BUILDING, 1891
(Royalty Coin)
423-431 East Commerce Street
James Riely Gordon

While not quite as exuberant as the Staacke and Stevens Buildings nearby, the Clifford Building shows Gordon's ability to work with an unusual and rather confined site. The rounded end that serves as a tower alongside the San Antonio River is a fine example of late 19th-century brickwork, with no ornate details to detract from the smooth curving masonry walls. The cupola atop the building provides an unexpected break from the mass of the structure. While the Clifford Building has acquired a coat of paint over its masonry surfaces, it has survived to this day with hardly any changes.

16 ★
STOCKMAN RESTAURANT, circa 1867
409 East Commerce Street
Renovated, 1972
Ford, Powell & Carson and Cy Wagner

The growing popularity of historic preservation moved in the early 1970s to old commercial buildings downtown, including these two venerable row structures. The real estate here along Commerce Street proved even more valuable because the buildings backed onto the River Walk with its daily throng of tourists and revelers. Thus, in the process of converting the high ceilings and expansive floor spaces to an Old-West-

theme restaurant, a major entry was created on the river side, three floors below street level. The interior was decorated with aged ranching paraphernalia and hand-crafted rustic furnishings. New concrete columns added for support were left unfinished.

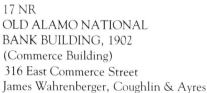

17 NR
OLD ALAMO NATIONAL
BANK BUILDING, 1902
(Commerce Building)
316 East Commerce Street
James Wahrenberger, Coughlin & Ayres

In 1916 architect Dielmann and engineers
figured that this 5-story steel-frame building—with brick veneer, Renaissance Revival details in granite, and a pressed metal
cornice—weighed 8000 tons. The estima-
tion was necessary to plan the building's
move of 16 feet 7 inches—accomplished
with jacks, wheels, and rails—for the widening of Commerce Street. The architect of
the top three stories in 1916 is unknown,
but the original cornice was evidently
replaced atop the new ninth floor.

18
CHARLES COURT, 1981-83
200 Block, South Presa Street
Tuggle & Graves

This lush and cozy court flanking the Old
Alamo National Bank building was once a
dead-end service alley for several buildings
facing Presa and Commerce streets.
During renovation of the site—which
includes the c. 1850 Batz House, the 1880
Pancoast Building by Alfred Giles (facade
removed in 1960), and the c. 1900 Texas
Hotel—the alley was made a principal
entrance for a new restaurant, offices,
shops, and residences in the buildings.

20 NR
STAACKE BROTHERS BUILDING,
1894
309 East Commerce Street
James Riely Gordon

19 NR
STEVENS BUILDING, 1891
315 East Commerce Street
Gordon & Laub
Renovated, 1983
Tuggle & Graves

John J. Stevens commissioned Gordon & Laub to build this Romanesque Revival edifice containing his office as well as commercial space. Eclectic facade details of round arches on columns, oriel windows, and balustraded parapet were executed in brick, limestone, and granite. Along with the adjacent Staacke Building, the facade was restored and the interior developed as contemporary office space in 1983.

The Brothers Staacke—August, Rudolph, and Herman—operated their thriving carriage business from this three-story brick structure and are credited with bringing the first automobile to the city in 1905. Architect Gordon utilized Texas red sandstone and red granite on the facade, detailed in Renaissance Revival motifs and complementing the adjacent Stevens Building he had designed three years before. In the recent renovation, alterations were removed, the exterior was water-blasted, and the interior was adapted to contemporary office space.

22 NR
SAN ANTONIO LOAN & TRUST BUILDING, 1903
235 East Commerce Street
Eidlitz & MacKenzie

21 NR
FIRST NATIONAL BANK, 1886
213 East Commerce Street
Cyrus L. W. Eidlitz

In this building, Eidlitz made some attempt at an appropriate response to the arid Texas climate by applying Moorish detailing from his eclectic vocabulary. The stepped-dome porch of the entry is supported by two polished-granite Moorish columns. The adjacent Syrian-arched window has a rectangular surround carved with Moorish motifs. Eidlitz's client, entrepreneur George Washington Brackenridge, had been a Union official during the Civil War, and returned to San Antonio as a victor after the war. The colonel flaunted his post-war prosperity with generous contributions to the city, and with this building for his bank, which held the pioneer national charter in Texas.

Col. George W. Brackenridge again employed architect Eidlitz when the banker's success called for expansion next to his 1886 San Antonio National Bank (213 East Commerce Street). But this time, regional trends were pushed aside by the national affection for Classicism, reflected in stone details and the pressed-metal cornice. The building now houses offices and private apartments.

Larry Pearlstone

Larry Pearlstone

25
MAIN PLAZA, from 1738
(Plaza de las Islas)

Canary Island immigrants arrived here in 1831 and began building their church facing this ground in 1738, establishing a public plaza as part of the grid-pattern street system they plotted. Troops of the presidio were garrisoned one block away, but the commander's office faced Main Plaza; here Apaches signed a peace treaty in 1749, then attacked with vengeance in 1789. Moses Austin proposed his Anglo colonization scheme to officials here in 1820; those colonists later fought a pitched battle with Mexican forces on this plaza in 1835, then holed up in the Alamo across the river. The new cathedral in 1868 and the courthouse in 1893 precipitated formal landscaping of the plaza, which remains an active public space.

23
ONE ALAMO CENTER, 1981
106 South St. Mary's Street
Ford, Powell & Carson

Built to house additional office space and a motor bank for the MBank Alamo, this eight-story rectangular block fills its site. Automobile traffic entirely dominates the open, brick-paved ground-floor level, with the exception of the shallow loggia facing South St. Mary's Street, where *Three-Way Piece #1: Points* by Henry Moore (1964) is sited. Continuous spandrels of precast concrete alternate with inset horizontal bands of bronze-tinted glazing. The corner bays are infilled with limestone panels.

24
ALAMO NATIONAL BANK
BUILDING, 1929
(MBank Alamo)
154 East Commerce Street
Graham, Anderson, Probst & White, Chicago
Renovated, 1976
Ford, Powell & Carson

The second home of one of the city's most prominent banking institutions, this structure is a rare example of the influence of an out-of-state firm on San Antonio architecture. As successor to the great D. H. Burnham, the Chicago firm of Graham, Anderson, Probst & White was among the leading practitioners of classicism in the design of high-rise office buildings. In this particular work, however, the detailing is spare.

26 NR
BEXAR COUNTY COURTHOUSE, 1896
Main Plaza
Gordon & Laub

James Riely Gordon was busy establishing himself as a prolific Texas courthouse architect when his partnership was commissioned in 1892 to design a building for Bexar County. His interpretations of the Romanesque style followed the national trend, and here he added other eclectic details in native Texas granite and sandstone. The massive segmental-arch entry is flanked by towers, one seven stories tall with a beehive spire. Numerous additions have altered the other elevations of the building, some in sympathy and others in opposition to Gordon & Laub's design and selection of materials.

27 ★ NR
SAN FERNANDO CATHEDRAL, 1749
114 Main Plaza
Nave and Facade, circa 1873
Francois Giraud
Restored, 1977
Ford, Powell & Carson

The oldest part of this church was begun in 1738 by Spanish Canary Island immigrants. The original cruciform plan was defined by rough limestone walls and a crossing dome. This configuration and facade were believed to be similar to an early church at Mission San Antonio de Valero (that church later collapsed and was replaced by the present Alamo church in 1744), with a central east entry and one bell tower. The present Gothic Revival edifice was begun in 1868, and incorporated a part of the original church connected to the new apse. During restoration, later additions were removed to reveal the c. 1749 walls and crossing dome.

28 NR
OLD FROST NATIONAL BANK
BUILDING, 1922
(Main Plaza Building)
103 Main Plaza
J.P. Haynes

The former home of the Frost National
Bank was the first 12-story office building in
San Antonio. While it pales in comparison
to the ruddy bulk of the Bexar County Courthouse across the square, the detailing merits
attention. Of special note are the round bas-
relief sculpture panels. Set between the dou-
ble-height arched window openings, they
are copies of U.S. coinage. The former
banking hall has been converted into a
cafeteria, a novel reuse that permitted the
space to retain its scale and elegance.

29 NR
SAN ANTONIO CITY HALL, 1891
Military Plaza
Otto Kramer, St. Louis/Chicago
Renovated, 1927
Adams & Adams

Originally exhibiting prominent Second
Empire elements, some of the building's
more subtle Renaissance Revival details
have survived extensive deterioration and
alteration. Walls are of smooth-cut limestone on a rusticated base. Aedicule windows, entablature courses, and other details
are also of limestone. All this embellish-
ment is credited to local stonemason Frank
Teich. The 1927 alterations lent a generally
Mediterranean air, inserting cast-stone
Romanesque arches in the central entries,
and substituting a fourth floor for a central
135-foot octagonal tower with mansard roof
and clock cupola. Conical turret roofs were
also removed.

30 NR
MILITARY PLAZA, from 1722
(Plaza de Armas)

Sited squarely in the middle of the former
drill ground of the Presidio de Bexar is the
ornate city hall of 1891. The military post
was established in 1722 to protect the
nearby missions along the San Antonio
River. The plaza was the site of public
executions after revolts in 1811 and 1813,
vigilante lynchings in the 1860s, and bustling market activities after the Civil War.
Only the Governor's Palace, facing the
courthouse block, and San Fernando
Church, with its old apse backing on the
site, survive from the days of an open plaza
that, with Main Plaza, functioned as the
heart of the city.

32 NR
VOGEL-BELT BUILDINGS,
1880-1888, 1891
111-121 Military Plaza
Renovated, 1979
Lance, Larcade & Bechtol

31 NR
SPANISH GOVERNOR'S PALACE,
1749
105 Military Plaza
Restored, 1930
Harvey P. Smith

Actually a residence and headquarters for the captain of the city's presidio, this one-story, flat-roofed adobe structure—with protruding *vigas*—received its popular name by tradition. After many years of neglect and alteration, the Spanish Colonial building was purchased by the city in 1929, and documented and restored during a rediscovery of San Antonio's architectural heritage. Smith eventually worked on most all of the missions and major Spanish Colonial structures remaining in and near the city.

A group of four commercial row buildings represents the late-19th-century commercial development of the old Military Plaza, in the city's traditional center. German immigrant Edward Steves built the first of these brick buildings facing the plaza in 1880. The Fashion Theater followed in 1884, designed by architect James Murphy. The last two buildings were built by Simon Fest in 1887. The present facades, unified with Italianate details, were constructed after the row was damaged in an 1891 fire.

33
LA CLEDE HOTEL, 1890
(San Antonio Metropolitan
 Health District)
322-344 West Commerce Street
Attributed to Alfred Giles

The key element here is streetscape, with
the building extending along West Commerce for 14 facade bays. Although the first-
floor fronts have been badly mistreated, the
upper floors have survived intact. The
monumental brick parapet unites the entire
composition, becoming more significant as
it approaches the centrally placed main
entrance to the structure. The attribution
of this structure to British-born Alfred
Giles is based upon stylistic grounds and is
not documented.

34 ★
NAVARRO HOUSE, circa 1850
228 South Laredo Street
Restored, 1962
Brooks Martin
Restored, 1979
Texas Parks & Wildlife Department

Three structures comprise this complex that
was the home and office of Jose Antonio
Navarro. The vernacular design of the *L*-
shaped house, the detached kitchen, and
two-story office represents practical construction of heavy stone walls and broad
frame porches. Navarro (1795-1871) was
one of two native Texans who signed the
state's Declaration of Independence from
Mexico in 1836 and assisted in drafting its
Constitution as a Republic.

35
EL MERCADO, 1976
500 Block, Produce Row
Martin & Ortega

In an attempt to revive the west end of
downtown, the city embarked upon an
ambitious scheme in 1973 to reuse the
blocky Market House Annex (1922, Leo
M.J. Dielmann) and the long, low, arcaded
Market House (1938, De Haven Pitts); con-
vert two blocks of Produce Row into a
pedestrian concourse; and rehabilitate the
one- and two-story brick, turn-of-the-cen-
tury storefronts along its south side. As
urban design, El Mercado demonstrates the
superiority of preservation and rehabilitation to demolition. Although gentrified
considerably, it is the surviving center of
urban intensity on the west side of
downtown.

Paul Hester

36
MILAM SQUARE, from 1808
Santa Rosa at Houston
Rehabilitated, 1976
James Keeter, Landscape Architect

The east end of this public space served as a cemetery for the Canary Island immigrants and their San Fernando church from 1808 to 1860. The grave markers were lost long ago, but rehabilitation in the 1970s placed symbolic headstones in the cemetery area and bronze plaques listing the burials recorded in the church books. An 1897 granite tombstone at the west end marks the burial site of Benjamin Rush Milam (1788-1835), a hero of the Texas Revolution who died leading the Siege of Bexar. During the 1936 Centennial a monument designed by architect Donald Nelson was added, topped by a 1937 bronze statue of Milam by sculptor Bonnie MacLeary.

37 NR
MENGER SOAP WORKS, 1850
500 North Santa Rosa Street
Restored (exterior) and adapted, 1970
Robert Callaway

Limestone rubble walls and rough-cut quoins and voussoirs enclose what is thought to be the oldest industrial building in Texas. This soap factory on San Pedro Creek was also possibly the first in the Southwest, and operated past the turn of the century. In 1970 apartments were built on the building's south side, and the veteran structure was converted to offices for the residential complex.

39 ★
RAND BUILDING, 1913
100 East Houston Street
Sanguinet & Staats, Fort Worth
Rehabilitated, 1982

38
ALAMEDA THEATER, 1949
314 West Houston Street
N. Strauss Nayfach

The last of San Antonio's great movie
palaces, the Alameda and its accompanying
four-story office block were built as a Mexican-American entertainment and professional center on what was then the Hispanic
end of the Houston Street retail district.
Nayfach's late-Modernistic design is totally
uninhibited, as the orange, green and blue
tile work, the aluminum arabesques, and
the unparalleled 86-foot-high illuminated
sign attest. The San Antonio Conservation
Society led a successful fight to stave off
demolition in 1982.

One of a series of tall buildings erected in
San Antonio to the designs of the early-
20th-century skyscraper kings of Texas, the
Rand Building combines Midwestern prog-
ressive composition and fenestration
with New York French classical ornamentation. The building originally housed the
Wolff & Marx department store at its base.
In 1981 the San Antonio Conservation
Society saved the building from demolition
and arranged its sale to Randstone Ventures,
for whom the Marmon Mok Partnership
restored the exterior and inserted a nine-
story glazed court that rises through the
center of the building.

41
HERTZBERG CLOCK, 1878
Northwest corner of Houston and
   St. Mary's
E. Howard Company, Boston
Moved, 1910

40
REPUBLICBANK PLAZA, 1985
175 East Houston Street
Ford, Powell & Carson and Fisher &
   Spillman

RepublicBank Plaza mitigates its sheer scale
and formal aloofness through several urban-
istic gestures: aligning the walls of the 13-
story, 300,000-square-foot office block with
Houston and St. Mary's streets; providing
sidewalk arcades; and configuring the office
block and the five-story banking pavilion (a

36-story, 800,000-square-foot tower will
complete the complex) around a mid-block
plaza linked to the River Walk. Against
considerable public protest, the Texas
Theater (1926, Boller Brothers) was
demolished to make way for the bank,
although the terra-cotta-adorned facade,
marquee, entrance bay, and ticket booth
remain standing in juxtaposition with the
new construction.

Considered by many to be the "official"
timepiece of downtown San Antonio, the
Hertzberg Clock originally served as func-
tional advertising for the Hertzberg Jewelry
Company. Of special interest is the fact that
the clock is a pre-electric device whose
works have to be hand-wound. The ring of
electric lights that serves to make the clock
readable at night is a more recent addition.

44 NR
MAJESTIC THEATER BUILDING, 1929
John Eberson
Rehabilitated, 1983
Barry Moore Architects, Inc., Houston

42
BOOK BUILDING, 1906
130 East Houston Street
Attributed to Dwight Book

The key to the character of the Book Build-ing is the consistent and dramatic use of round-arched window bays on the street facades. The scale of these openings results in an unusual, almost airy, look to the outer skin. Dwight Dana Book, a civil engineer and U.S. Army officer, was probably capa-ble of designing a building, and research has not located a more logical attribution for the author of the design.

43
GUNTER HOTEL, 1909
205 East Houston Street
Mauran, Russell & Garden, St. Louis
Addition of 9th-11th floors, 1927

The Gunter is the first in a long line of hotels erected in Texas to the designs of Mauran, Russell & Garden (later known as Mauran, Russel & Crowell), which include the Rice Hotel in Houston, the Galvez Hotel in Galveston, and the Blackstone Hotel in Fort Worth. The original design, with its multistory three-sided bays and terra-cotta-decorated base floors, is a good example of the "Chicago-style" high rise. The enclosure of the mezzanine-level veran-dah provided much-needed additional din-ing seating.

In the heyday of vaudeville and early movies, the "atmospheric theater" was the last word in entertainment. Illusions of clouds and stars in the ceiling combined with cleverly lit architectural vignettes flanking the stage to transport the theater-goer to another world. Air conditioning gave a final boost of comfort and fascination to the performance. Eberson, one of the most prolific theater designers of his era, called upon the Spanish and Moorish herit-age of San Antonio for the elaborate detail-ing of the Majestic's interior. The auditorium occupies six levels of the accom-panying steel-frame, 18-story office building.

45 ★ NR
CENTRAL TRUST COMPANY
BUILDING, 1919
(South Texas Building)
603 Navarro Street
Sanguinet & Staats, Fort Worth
Rehabilitated, 1982
The Benham Group

The Fort Worth architects designed this 12-story structure for Central Trust with a steel frame and veneers of brick, green granite, and terra cotta. At that time it was billed as the finest building in town and the most expensive bank building in Texas. In 1932 the name was changed to South Texas Building, and in 1947 the Ayres firm designed alterations for the first three floors. The building was rehabilitated as office space in 1982.

46
KRESS BUILDING, 1938
315 East Houston Street
Edward F. Sibbert

Sibbert, Kress's vice president in charge of architecture, endowed his five-story San Antonio store with attributes employed in many of the Kress stores he designed during the 1930s—an Art-Deco-style storefront sheathed in terra cotta in shades of dull pink, yellow, green, and copper. The scrolled pediments atop the corner bays and the Modernistic vertical fluting between window bays are thick, heavy, and flat. Kress's sign is a '30s hallmark. Architecturally integrated, it is oriented to the flow of traffic along Houston Street.

48
HYATT REGENCY HOTEL, 1981
123 Losoya Street
Thompson, Ventulett, Stainback &
    Associates and Ford, Powell & Carson

This 16-story, 633-room hotel, designed by
the Atlanta architect Raymond F. Stainback, is wrapped around an obligatory Hyatt
"atrium" lobby, which here contains a public thoroughfare, the Paseo del Alamo. The
lobby court is expressed on the west by a
glass curtain wall shielded by rows of bright
red canopies set in a delicate network of
steel webbing and providing a welcome note
of texture and color. Approached from the
north, along Broadway-Losoya, the Hyatt's
dazzlingly white, poured-in-place concrete
mass looms up like an iceberg in the midst
of the city. From other vantage points, however, it is surprisingly unobtrusive. Across
Losoya, between the Paseo and Houston
Street, lies the Hyatt Garage with its con-
textually attentive, ground-floor retail
arcade.

47
G. BEDELL MOORE BUILDING, 1904
(110 Broadway)
Houston at Broadway
Atlee B. Ayres
Renovated, 1984
Urban Design Group, Tulsa

This is one of Atlee B. Ayres's earliest commercial buildings, and one of the most
enjoyable. The composition of the facade
designs, with round-arched window bays
framing three stories, is standard for the
period, but the extensive use of ornamental
terra cotta represents a significant development on the local scene. The building was
evidently a business success as well since the
sixth floor was added five years after the
completion of the structure. The architect
maintained his office in this building for 20
years, before moving to a later masterpiece,
the Smith-Young Tower. Recent remodeling included a skylighted atrium.

49
CHANDLER BUILDING, 1895
110 East Crockett Street
Charles A. Coughlin
Renovated, 1961
Brooks Martin
Renovated, 1986
Humberto Saldana & Associates

A small but well-designed office block, the Chandler Building is one of the few surviving works of Coughlin, who was to become the partner of Atlee B. Ayres before Coughlin's untimely death in 1905. While Coughlin's original work is still evident, the building was altered significantly by remodeling (one of the first on the Paseo del Rio) that removed the original fenestration of the first-floor round-arched openings. Current renovation will restore much of the original design.

50 NR
CASINO CLUB BUILDING
102 West Crockett Street
Kelwood Company

A triangular lot on the San Antonio River was developed with this clubhouse and office for a large social club. The six-story Art Deco structure is clad with brick and cast-stone trim detailed in Mayan reliefs. The Casino Club sold the building in 1940 to Oklahoma oil entrepreneur Thomas Gilcrease as his headquarters. Since 1952 the building has been frequently vacant, but is now in use as apartments and retail.

51
NIX PROFESSIONAL BUILDING, 1929
410 Navarro Street
Henry T. Phelps

This is an interesting case of architectural masquerading in which a hospital is imitating an office building. The glory of the Nix is its wonderful coat of polychrome terracotta ornament, the best single collection of the material in all of San Antonio. Most structures associated with the practice of medicine are far less inviting than the Nix,

52
LA MANSION DEL RIO HOTEL, 1968
112 College Street
Wallace B. Thomas
Alterations and additions, 1979
Harwood K. Smith & Partners, Dallas

Built on the site of St. Mary's School, the hotel complex incorporates at its center the school's original building of 1857 by Francois P. Giraud. Like Giraud's buildings at the Ursuline Academy, the school bespoke its frontier situation in the barren, almost factory-like quality of its massing, proportions, and fenestration (a quality that was altered considerably with the addition of

balconies, an attic-level Mansard roof, and an arched entrance portal.) As a hotel, La Mansion is a romantic architectural invention, evoking a Spanish-colonial past too charming to have been true. Wallace Thomas organized the six-story, 200-room hotel around a central patio. Along the River Walk he faceted planes of inset and projecting balconies to conform to the course of the stream. Thus the hotel does not overwhelm the River Walk by its considerable bulk. Formerly La Posada, the hotel was transformed into La Mansion del Rio by the Dallas architects Harwood K. Smith & Partners, who intelligently adopted and maintained Thomas's organization, massing, and details. Extensive interior alterations of 1985 are by Ford, Powell & Carson.

54
ST. ANTHONY HOTEL, 1909
300 East Travis Street
J. Flood Walker
Alterations and additions, 1936
John M. Marriott
Alterations and additions, 1941
Fred S. Jones

The St. Anthony, as it exists today, is largely the result of Marriott's 1936 remodeling, in which he transformed Walker's two, blocky, free-standing towers into a single building; Jones's addition of the east wing resulted in a simple extension of Marriott's elevations. Walker, a transplanted Californian, capped his towers with colossally scaled shaped gables and projecting tiled cornices. There was a "Mexican patio" and, along the Travis Park front, an open-air, ground-floor loggia. Central air conditioning (1936) and a six-level parking garage (1941) were advance features of the two sets of additions. The hotel was rehabilitated in 1983 by Chumney, Jones & Kell, with public spaces restored to their appearances of 1936.

53
TRAVIS PARK UNITED METHODIST CHURCH, 1886
20 East Travis Street
Francis Crider
Addition 1902
Harvey L. Page

Travis Park Methodist Church houses the city's oldest Methodist congregation in a building that has been the subject of numerous additions and alterations over the years. The original block, with the cylindrical tower, was constructed by the builder Francis Crider, a member of the congregation. The church was enlarged by Harvey L. Page, whose design extended the facade along Navarro Street and included a large auditorium. Due to a major fire in October of 1955, little of the original interior has survived intact. While Travis Park Methodist is not the architectural equal of St. Mark's Episcopal across the park, it is nevertheless important in maintaining the 19th-century scale of the park and its environs.

55
TRAVIS PARK, circa 1870
300 East Travis Street
Renovated, 1985
O'Neill & Perez

The land for this early municipal park was
the orchard of Samuel Maverick, who
willed the site to the city in 1870. Maverick
had been elected by his comrades at the
nearby Alamo in February, 1836, to represent them at the independence convention
at Washington-on-the-Brazos. He missed
the subsequent slaughter of the Alamo
defenders on March 6, but returned here
after the war and bought a homestead near
where his friends had fallen. In 1900 the
United Daughters of the Confederacy
donated the central monument—designed
by Virginia Montgomery and sculpted in
1899 by noted craftsman Frank Teich—and
the two Confederate cannon. The park was
saved from demolition in 1954.

56
ST. MARK'S EPISCOPAL CHURCH,
1875
315 East Pecan Street
Richard Upjohn
Additions 1948-49
Henry Steinbomer

Although it has been enlarged and is now
flanked by numerous other structures
required by the congregation, St. Mark's
still carries the signature of its original architect. Upjohn was one of the foremost
church architects of the 19th century.
Closely linked to the early stages of the
Gothic Revival and the New York
Ecclesiological Society, he saw reform of
church design as a means of improving both
architecture and the practice of religion. The
church presents some interesting contrasts;
the exterior, for example, is dominated by
the power of the heavy limestone walls,
while the interior has a much lighter feeling
conveyed by its timber framing. The massing of the east end of the church's exterior,
with its small bell cote, is outstanding.

57
INTERFIRST PLAZA, 1984
300 Convent Street
Skidmore, Owings & Merrill, Houston

The first high rise of any consequence to be
built in downtown San Antonio in several
years, InterFirst takes some design hints
from the city's fine stock of 1920s and '30s
towers. The step-back massing gives the
building a distinctive profile, but it is the
pleated character of the walls that lends an
air of drama to the design. The effect of a
sunset on the building is truly remarkable as
the light transforms it into monumental
sculpture. The main banking lobby is an
effective interior space, large in scale and
detailed with none of the overblown
extravagance that so often accompanies
contemporary bank interiors.

58
SOUTHWESTERN BELL TELEPHONE
BUILDING, 1931
105 Auditorium Circle
I.R. Timlin

What remains intact of the original at
street-level, after conspicuous alterations
and additions, is the glorious terra-cotta
decoration with which Timlin, the St.
Louis-based corporate architect for Southwestern Bell, festooned the first three floors
of the building. The portal of Mission San
Jose provided an ostensible point of departure for this riot of free-flowing Spanish
Baroque ornament. Contextual urbanisti-
cally as well as stylistically, the Southwestern
Bell Building conforms to its polygonal site;
Timlin chamfered the symmetrical east elevation in deference to the adjoining Municipal Auditorium.

59 NR
MUNICIPAL AUDITORIUM, 1926
100 Auditorium Circle
Atlee B. Ayres & Associates
Restored, 1985
Phelps/Garza/Bomberger

Fully accepted as a regional favorite by the
1920s, the Spanish Colonial Revival was
deemed the appropriate stylistic expression
for this important civic building. The
auditorium's main entry arcade is flanked by
domed towers and highlighted with carved
Indiana limestone details and decorative
tiles, all a veneer over a reinforced-concrete
structure. The steel frames of the sprawling
auditorium dome and 90-foot-high flyloft
were rebuilt after a 1979 fire, and the entire
building was proudly restored to its role of a
vital activity center for the city.

60
MAVERICK-CARTER HOUSE, 1894
119 Taylor Street
Alfred Giles

The most monumental house extant in San
Antonio by Giles, the Maverick-Carter
house was built for William Maverick and
in 1910 was sold to H. C. and Aline Badger
Carter. Mrs. Carter, a noted astronomer
and Texas poet-laureate, added the roof-top
observatory. The design of the house represents a mix of Romanesque forms and those
more commonly used in the 1870s and
1880s. The plan is a simple rectangle with
projecting bays. Most openings are rectangular, with massive stone lintels and sills,
except for the round-arched quasi-Palladian
window on the second floor over the main
entrance.

61
BARR BUILDING, 1912
213-219 Broadway Street
Leo M.J. Dielmann

A conspicuous structure on Broadway by
virtue of its size and unusual detailing, the
Barr Building was designed by Dielmann to
serve the needs of a special client—photog-
rapher David Perry Barr, for whom the
building served as studio and residence. The
lower level was leased out to tenants, and
Barr's studio was set to the rear of the second
floor. The north-facing skylight, which was
reconstructed during rehabilitation,
provided ample natural lighting. The inset
balcony of the Broadway elevation indicates
the location of the owner's residence, overlooking the street. Dielmann, who made a
reputation as a church architect, also produced a number of small-scale commercial
buildings in the city, most of which no
longer survive.

62
SCOTTISH RITE TEMPLE, 1924
308 Avenue E
Herbert M. Greene Co.
Ralph Cameron, supervising architect

Designed in a manner befitting the ancient
heritage of the Masonic orders, the Scotish
Rite Temple in Washington, D.C., which
was a literal copy of the Mausoleum at
Halicarnassus. Greene's interpretation,
perhaps a result of a desire to keep costs
down, does not feature Pope's peripteral col-
onnade around the upper section of the
building. The quality of the detailing
remains high, however, with outstanding
metal work affixed to the main elevation.
The most important decorative elements
are the monumental bronze outer doors,
which feature George Washington as their
central iconographic motif executed by the
noted San Antonio sculptor Pompeo
Coppini. This is one of the city's best
works from the 1920s.

63
FIRST PRESBYTERIAN CHURCH, 1909
408 North Alamo Street
Atlee B. Ayres

In spite of his long and prolific career in San
Antonio, Atlee B. Ayres did not receive
numerous commissions for churches. On
the basis of its exterior, First Presbyterian
suggests that the architect was perhaps not
truly comfortable dealing with the problems
of church design, as it is not an imaginative
work, and one which in fact was never completed according to the plans. The loss of
the spires that would have topped the
church towers makes the structure seem
heavier than intended. The interior, on the
other hand, is very fine, containing some
monumental wood framing work in the
auditorium.

64 NR
SULLIVAN CARRIAGE HOUSE, 1896
314 Fourth Street
Alfred Giles

Giles accomplished an impressive, one- and
two-story interpretation of Richardsonian
Romanesque with this auxiliary structure
for banker Daniel J. Sullivan's 1885 mansion. The mansion was replaced by a news-
paper plant around 1965, but the stable and
carriage house of rusticated limestone
remains virtually intact on the interior. One
of the few surviving fragments from what
was once an affluent residential area, the
building is threatened by surrounding commercial expansion, and several schemes to
move it or rebuild it elsewhere have been
discussed recently.

65
YWCA BUILDING, 1909
(South Texas Regional Blood Bank)
318 McCullough
Atlee B. Ayres
Remodeled, 1984
The Marmon Mok Partnership

Originally constructed to house the city's
YWCA, this rather restrained Renaissance
Revival design was subject to a dramatic
transformation so as to accommodate its
new function. The once-open forecourt was
enclosed in a light frame of glass and steel,
making it still possible to read the original
design. The two flanking wings are now
connected by pedestrian bridges that allow
unobstructed views down into the
former entry court and out to the street.

66 ★ NR
OLD LONE STAR BREWERY, 1904
(San Antonio Museum of Art)
110 West Jones Avenue
E. Jugenfeld & Co. and
    Wahrenberger & Beckmann
Adapted, 1981
Cambridge Seven, Cambridge, Mass.
Associated Architects:
    Martin & Ortega
Chumney, Jones & Kell

Buildings of various functions for the brewing of beer, with heights ranging from two
to five stories, were unified with crenelated
projections and other corbelled brick
details. Jugenfeld was a St. Louis-based firm
specializing in breweries; Wahrenberger &
Beckmann were the local supervising architects. Around 1900, brewer Adolphus

Busch invested in the Lone Star company
and served as its president for several years.
The company built a new brewery in 1957
and abandoned this complex. In 1980 an
unusual adaptive-use program developed
the interior as a spacious contemporary
museum, while preserving the exterior
appearance with few alterations. A skylighted central entrance space is flanked on
either side by the east and west gallery
towers, which have been joined by a
glassed-in bridge above. Elevators in each
tower afford floor-to-floor gallery previews
through glass cabs. A roof terrace atop the
east tower offers expansive views of the city.

67
CLAUDIUS KING HOUSE, 1880
(Bright Shawl)
819 Augusta Street
Alfred Giles

The *L*-plan cottage is an important house type in central Texas, where it is often constructed of limestone masonry. This example by Giles is perhaps more ambitious than most in terms of its detailing, including the bay that projects out of the face of the *L*. The massive scale of the limestone blocks belies the small size of the house. Restored by the San Antonio Junior League, the house has unfortunately lost a portion of its large grounds to surface parking.

68 ★
CENTRAL YMCA, 1972
903 North St. Mary's Street
Marmon & Mok Associates

A one- and two-story structure of poured-in-place warm-toned concrete construction, the building has projecting bays that contain deep-set windows and planting troughs. Vertical scoring differentiates wall surfaces from smooth-finished, horizontally articulated floor and roof slabs.

69
MADISON SQUARE PRESBYTERIAN
CHURCH, 1895
319 Camden Street
Architect unknown

Seemingly out of place in a rapidly changing neighborhood, Madison Square Presbyterian is a reminder of what was once one of the more appealing residential sections of the late 19th-century city. While there is no solid evidence to support it, the church design may be the work of James Wahrenberger, for the bold forms of the church tower resemble other of his works. The congregation played a major role in the city's 20th-century architectural history by aiding in the 1942 relocation of Trinity University here from its campus in Waxahachie.

70 ★
MAIN BANK AND TRUST, 1960
911 North Main Avenue
Reginald Roberts Associates and
Kuehne, Brooks & Barr, Austin

A clean-lined pavilion set on a low podium,
this small bank building exemplifies the late
50s predilection for industrial delicacy.
Steel columns supporting the overhanging
roof slab are cantilevered beyond the foundation to enhance the illusion that the
building floats effortlessly above its parking
lot. Decorative metal grilles fixed to the columns screen the bank's curtain walls on the
east and west.

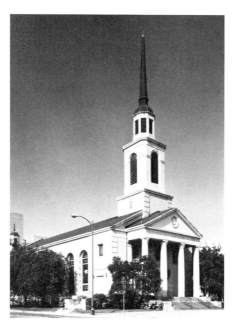

71
CENTRAL CHRISTIAN CHURCH,
  1950
720 North Main Avenue
Henry Steinbomer

As an architect especially identified with
churches, Steinbomer is best represented by
the Central Christian Church. For its
design he appropriated the familiar image of
the neoclassical church with temple-front
portico and spire-topped bell tower;
simplified the details considerably; and
reproduced it in the characteristic San
Antonio materials of tan brick and limestone. The vertically accentuated symmetry
of the church's principal elevation and the
graceful row of long, arched windows along
its western flank are especially effective in
fixing the building to its pivotal site.

72
BANCO DE SAN ANTONIO, 1976
1 Romana Plaza
O'Neill & Perez and Lance & Larcade

This long, thin three-story building is an
architectural exposition of precast concrete
construction. Trays of office space are
stacked above covered parking on the
ground floor, allowing the building to fill
out its narrow, but highly visible, site. The
gray monochrome of the concrete surfaces
provides a neutral counterpoint to the tan
tapestry brick walls of the adjacent Sears,
Roebuck & Company department store of
1929.

74
LEFT BANK CONDOMINIUMS, 1979
701 North St. Mary's Street
Jack L. Duffin

This 24-unit, low-rise condominium apartment project presents two distinct faces. To the north, facing the Ursuline Academy and the San Antonio River, it is articulated as a succession of vertical unit fronts, faceted to conform to the river's course. Toward the south it becomes an activated composition of shadowed balconies and horizontal stucco parapets. Adroit handling of grade separations between the River Walk and north-facing gardens assures privacy.

73 ★ NR
OLD URSULINE ACADEMY AND
CONVENT, from 1851
(Southwest Craft Center)
300 Augusta Street
attributed to Jules Poinsard
Additions, after 1866
Francois Giraud
Renovated, 1975
Martin & Ortega
Renovated, 1977-86
Ford, Powell & Carson

Nuns from the Ursuline order in New Orleans established a high school for girls at this site in 1851. The original academy building was constructed of *pise de terre*, or rammed earth, a technique familiar to Poinsard. Walls were built by packing an earthen mix between a shallow wooden form, which was moved up as the wall was built higher. The academy thrived after the Civil War, and five large buildings were added to the complex, built of limestone blocks and detailed with Gothic and Renaissance Revival elements. The clock tower on one building is a familiar landmark along the San Antonio River. The complex now serves as the Southwest Craft Center, and houses Club Giraud, a private social club which benefits the craft center.

75 ★
NBC CENTER DRIVE-IN BANK, 1976
430 Soledad Street
The Marmon Mok Partnership

A ten-level parking garage, an eight-story office building, and a motor bank pavilion comprise this group of structures, located on two blocks and focused on the 21-story National Bank of Commerce Building (1957, Kenneth Franzheim and Atlee B. & Robert M. Ayres). Franzheim, a Houston architect, acknowledged San Antonio tradition by encasing his tower in tan brick and limestone. Marmon Mok retained this tawny color scheme in their precast concrete garage and office building. The motor bank, sheltered beneath a dark, steel, space-frame canopy, is treated as a sculptural element in the midst of the taller surrounding structures.

76
MILAM BUILDING, 1928
115 East Travis Street
George Willis

Once the tallest reinforced concrete building in the world, the Milam Building reflects the trend toward high-rise massing that was being set in New York skyscrapers of the 1920s. The decidedly blocky form of the structure, with its U-shaped central court, is most effective from a distance. The sidewalk elevations are kept rather plain, the vaguely Spanish Renaissance-inspired ornament being confined to the upper floors and the top of the 21-story central tower.

77
PLAZA HOTEL, 1927
(Granada Hotel)
311 South St. Mary's Street
Atlee B. & Robert M. Ayres

Given the dominance of San Antonio's Spanish heritage, it is not surprising to find that the large hotels of the early 20th century adopted architectural forms and details evoking that past. Designed by the city's most important and prolific firm of the 1920s and '30s, the Plaza was constructed in two stages. While somewhat austere on the exterior, the hotel's interior contains some extremely fine detailing, including ceilings that seem to derive from Mudejar-style work in Spain during the 15th century.

78
SMITH-YOUNG TOWER, 1929
(Tower Life Building)
310 South St. Mary's Street
Atlee B. & Robert M. Ayres

For nearly 30 years the tallest structure in
San Antonio, the octagonal Smith-Young
Tower is still one of the city's most commanding works. The exterior features a mix
of brick- and terra-cotta details, with the
Gothic-spirited ornament fitting neatly into
the set-back upper floors.

79
OLD FEDERAL RESERVE BANK
BUILDING, 1928
127 Navarro Street
Atlee B. & Robert M. Ayres

Considering the client, this is an unusually
inviting piece of architecture. At the time
of its design, most Federal Reserve branches
were considerably more monumental and
intimidating, but this specimen looks more
like the branch of a local commercial bank.
The importance of the institution is still
expressed through the granite used on the
exterior, most conspicuously on the Ionic
columns set in antis by the main entrance.
This sort of quiet dignity is altogether appropriate for the building's present occupant,
the Consulate of Mexico.

80
GRESSER-HAYS HOUSE, circa 1870
225 South Presa Street

While once a major feature of the core of
the city, houses of this type have become
scarce, vanishing with the more intense
development that began in the 1880s. The
detailing of the street facade is marked by
particularly fine French doors and casement
windows, which served to open up the
rooms to the shade of the front verandah.
The present house was erected by Louis
Gresser, probably incorporating portions of
an earlier residence located on the site.

Rick Gardner

Tony Weisgarber

82
ARNESON RIVER THEATER, 1939
San Antonio River Walk
Robert H.H. Hugman

This bend in the river had been a dumping ground for numerous automobile repair shops occupying the riverbank before its redevelopment during the Depression. With a grant from the Work Projects Administration (WPA), the city removed tons of auto scraps and laid out amphitheater seating on one bank facing a stage on the opposite bank. Ed Arneson was a local engineer directing the WPA district office. The bells originally envisioned by Hugman were finally cast by the Alamo Iron Works and installed in 1978.

81 ★ NR
LA VILLITA, 1792
Bounded by Durango, Navarro, and Alamo
   Streets and the San Antonio River
Restored, 1939-41
O'Neil Ford
Restored, 1980
Saldana, Williams & Schubert and
   Ford, Powell & Carson
PLAZA NACIONAL, 1976 ★
William Parrish

Once a Coahuiltecan village, this habitable site on a bend of the San Antonio River was first occupied by Europeans in 1768. It served as mission land for the Alamo and was first named La Villita in 1792. The cluster of some 27 buildings represents continued occupation for more than 200 years. Early Spanish and Mexican houses were built of stuccoed adobe brick and caliche. Later cut-stone vernacular structures were built by German settlers, including the 1876 church. Beginning in 1939, there was a cooperative effort of the city, the fledgling San Antonio Conservation Society, and the National Youth Administration to clean up the area and restore it as a public center. Restoration consultant O'Neil Ford set the tone of authenticity that makes La Villita seem like a real place. In 1974, a hodgepodge of five structures owned by the Joykist Candy Company were purchased and subsequently were restored by William Parrish. This award-winning complex at Nueva Street and South Presa is known as Plaza Nacional. Recent efforts at La Villita include structural repairs and refurbishing, and new restroom facilities, lighting, landscaping, paving, and signage.

83 ★
LA VILLITA ASSEMBLY HALL, 1959
401 Villita Street
O'Neil Ford & Associates

A modest building set in the midst of La Villita, the Assembly Hall reflects Ford's belief that a straightforward acknowledgment of structure and materials was more faithful to the spirit of the place than stylistic revival. The program suggested a cylindrically shaped building. This, in turn, occasioned the use of a steel-cable roof suspension system with a clear span 132 feet in diameter. Ford and his associate N.A. Salas surfaced the concave roof and the upper walls of the steel-framed assembly hall with precast panels; the lower walls and the courtyard enclosures are of Mexican brick. Landscape architect Stewart E. King, with James Keeter, laid out the patio garden, onto which the central space of the assembly hall opens. Ford's brother, Lynn, handcrafted the ceramic medallions mounted near the entry.

84
OLD SAN ANTONIO PUBLIC
LIBRARY, 1930
(Hertzberg Circus Collection)
210 West Market Street
Herbert S. Green
Restored 1971
Brooks Martin and Associates

This building, now home to the Hertzberg Circus Collection, San Antonio's finest example of Modern classicism as espoused by Bertram Grosvenor Goodhue. While not on the same level as Goodhue's Nebraska State Capitol, the manner in which Green pared down his ornamental details clearly owes a debt to Goodhue's masterpiece. The main entrance arch, notable for the two robed figures rising from the masonry of the flanking buttresses, is the focus of most of the detailing. Happily, when the library moved to new quarters, none of the external iconography was removed, leaving Ralph Waldo Emerson's words above the front door to remind us of what was once housed within.

85 ★
HILTON PALACIO DEL RIO HOTEL,
1968
200 South Alamo Street
Cerna & Garza

Notable as a demonstration of engineering and technical ingenuity, the 21-story, 500-room hotel was built in a nine-month time period by general contractor H.B. Zachry to accommodate visitors to HemisFair 68. The fifth through the 20th floors consist of individual, reinforced concrete, modular room units trucked to the site fully furnished and equipped, then hoisted into place to either side of the slip-formed elevator core.

HemisFair

HemisFair, the 1968 world's fair honoring San Antonio's 250th birthday, served as impetus for a vast urban renewal project covering 92.6 acres north of the city center and costing $156 million. A branch of the San Antonio River and walkway was diverted into the plaza grounds, and several hotels were constructed nearby. More than six million visitors crowded Hemis-Fair during its six months of operation in 1968. Many of the facilities remaining were part of the exhibit buildings constructed by some 25 nations, plus the $6.75 million U.S. Pavilion (now the John H. Wood Courthouse and Federal Building), the $10 million Texas Pavilion (now the Institute of Texan Cultures), and the $5.5 million Tower of the Americas. Several historic structures from the renewal area were clustered and utilized as fair buildings. Today the plaza features the convention center arena and concert hall; a campus of the University of Mexico and the Instituto Cultural Mexicano; Texas A&M University's Engineering School Extension Service and South Central Regional Training Center; the Witte Museum's Transportation exhibit; and the San Antonio Park Police headquarters.

86
TOWER OF THE AMERICAS, 1968
HemisFair Plaza
Ford, Powell & Carson

Built as the centerpiece of HemisFair 68, the 622-foot-high tower is still the tallest structure in San Antonio. Six levels of pub-licly-accessible restaurant and observation decks rotate—one revolution per hour—atop the cylindrical, slip-formed concrete spindle. Collaborating with Boone Powell on the design of the Tower of the Americas was the Spanish-Mexican engineer Felix Candela.

87
SCHULTZE'S STORE, 1891
300 HemisFair Plaza

The reworking of downtown San Antonio for HemisFair spared the Schultze Store, now the Melodrama Playhouse & Saloon. The finely detailed structure is one of the few surviving small-scale Italianate com-mercial buildings in the city. Efforts to pre-serve the building attracted much popular attention and support, partly because of its locally manufactured cast-iron work and milled woodwork, as well as the pressed-metal cornice reportedly made by the Schultze firm.

HemisFair

89 ★
UNITED STATES PAVILION—
CONFLUENCE THEATER, 1967
(John H. Wood, Jr., United States
Courthouse)
655 East Durango Street
Marmon Mok & Associates

88
INSTITUTE OF TEXAN CULTURES,
1968
801 South Bowie Street
Caudill Rowlett Scott and Callins &
    Wagner

Several tendencies current in American
architecture in the late 1960s converge in
the Institute of Texan Cultures building,
constructed by the State of Texas for Hemis-
Fair 68 and now operated as an exhibition
and research center. Heavy, sculptural
massing; constructivist minimalism in
exposed limestone aggregate concrete; and
camouflaging the building's form with
earthen berms were all essayed here by the
Houston architects CRS. The entrance

way—a broad, granite-paved causeway that
spans a chanelled, granite water garden—
impresses. But the neutral, artificially-lit,
loft-like exhibition space inside contains
no architectural climax, the big, honey-
combed hollow for multi-image media
presentations notwithstanding.

Designed as the United States Pavilion at
HemisFair, the structure has since been
converted to a Federal Courthouse. The use
of travertine creates a formal presence made
less formidable by the somewhat unexpected glass walls. Noteworthy are the great
pains taken in matching up the veining of
the travertine, as well as the slightly
unnerving thinness of the peripteral
columns.

90
ALDERETE HOUSES, circa 1818, 1850
526 East Nueva Street
Restored, 1982

These two structures stand as lingering examples of the earliest Hispanic building techniques. The rear house is presumed that of Dolores Alderete, who held a Spanish land grant for the property c.1818. It is of *palisado* construction, with walls of vertical poles laced together and plastered with a mud mixture. The front house was built c.1850 as a two-room residence of stuccoed-stone walls, with two rooms added in the late 1800s. Both houses are now roofed with standing-seam sheet metal, and have been converted to an apartment and an office, respectively.

91
OLD GERMAN-ENGLISH SCHOOL,
1859, 1869, circa 1875
419 South Alamo Street
G. Friesleben, J.H. Kampmann
Renovated, 1964-68
Allison B. Peery
Renovated, 1982
Ford, Powell & Carson

These one- and two-story buildings represent the later German presence on the edge of the old La Villita quarter. Two parallel pavilions define a pleasant court now landscaped with live oak trees. The old school is built of heavy limestone rubble walls and adapted to the temperate climate with shading galleries facing the court. Standing-seam metal roofs are typical of late-19th-century practice. The complex now serves as a conference center for the nearby Four Seasons Hotel.

92
STAFFEL/ELMENDORF/TYLER
HOUSE, circa 1850
220 Arciniega Street
Restored, 1979
Ford, Powell & Carson

German immigrants to San Antonio combined their own building experience with details they observed on existing Texas structures. Their resulting residences were typically one-story stuccoed-stone construction, with central halls and porches learned from their New World-neighbors. This surviving example was purchased after 1865 by Heine and Adeline Staffel and occupied by their descendants, Elmendorfs and Tylers, into the 20th century. It was restored as a facility of the Four Seasons Hotel and now is part of its inner court.

93
DIAZ HOUSE, circa 1840
206 Arciniega Street
Restored, 1980
Ford, Powell & Carson

This vernacular residence built of stuccoed stone exhibits a symmetrical plan, but with separate entrances and no central hall. Two inner hearths are arranged centrally and back-to-back, resulting in a "saddlebag" configuration. Few openings and small windows indicate an early "passive solar" awareness, allowing the thick stone walls and their slow heat gain to keep the house cool in the typically hot climate. Simple molding on the porch columns alludes to the popular Greek Revival detailing on finer homes of the time. The house is now part of the Four Seasons Hotel complex.

94 ★
FOUR SEASONS HOTEL, 1979
555 South Alamo Street
Ford, Powell & Carson

In this design the architects sought to reintroduce the particularity of scale, texture, and detail lost when this sector of the city was desolated by urban renewal clearance during the middle 1960s. Taking advantage of the generous 4-1/2 acre site, they designed a "garden hotel," a four-, five- and six-story building which serves as a backdrop for the landscaped outdoor spaces around which it is configured. Shallowly-pitched ridge roofs surfaced with standing-seam metal, tiers of metal verandas, and the stucco finish of the precast concrete walls insinuate a kinship with the houses of La Villita to the north. The gardens, however, are the major focus of attention. Fountains, terraces, pergolas, and a swimming pool are interspersed with lush plantings. Three small mid-19th-century houses that survived on the site and the more substantial buildings of the German-English School also were incorporated into the complex.

58

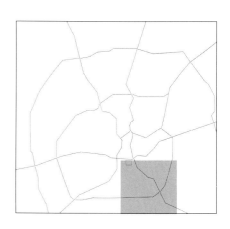

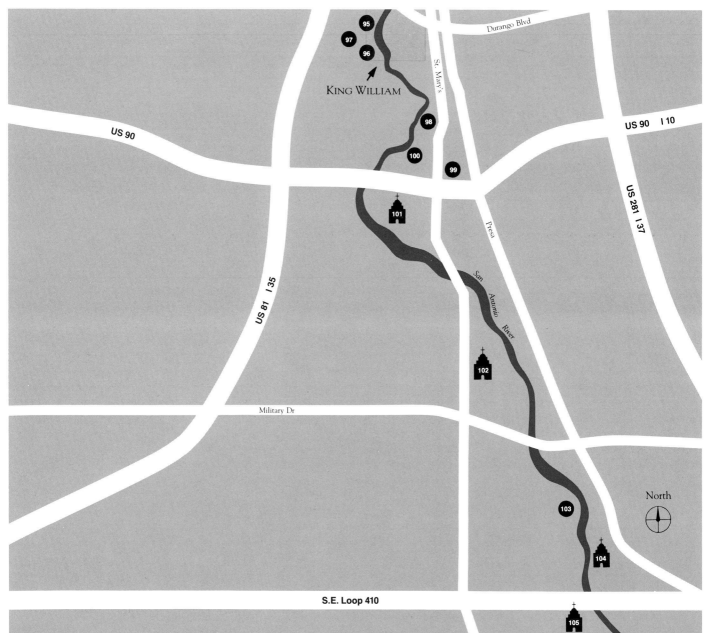

Durango Blvd

St. Mary's

US 90

US 90 **I 10**

95

97

96

KING WILLIAM

98

100

99

US 281 I 37

US 81 I 35

Presa

San Antonio River

101

102

Military Dr

North

103

104

S.E. Loop 410

105

South

One of the more remarkable features of San Antonio is the extent to which one can still grasp some sense of what the landscape was like when the first Mexican soldiers and Franciscan priests arrived here in 1718. Of course, this glimpse of the past is only possible in connection with the famed San Antonio missions, which are the dominant presence of the south side of the city.

For all of the 18th century, and until the final secularization of the mission lands by 1824, all of the territory one passes through along the Mission Trail was allocated to the five missions: San Antonio de Valero, Concepcion, San Jose, San Juan, and Espada. Each of the missions maintained lands that were used as *labores*, or tilled and irrigated fields, and *pasturas*, pasture land for the use of the mission livestock. While the secularization of the mission lands did bring some new residents to the area, it was still a major trip in the 1880s to visit the two most distant missions, San Juan and Espada, which were considered an overnight excursion from the center of the city. The only segment of the mission lands that was to be developed in the 19th century is known today as the King William District. Once a part of the lands of San Antonio de Valero, King William was the first true surburban addition to the city, and its architectural character is dominated by the large-scale villas that reflect the teachings of Andrew Jackson Downing, as well as the desire of the wealthier members of San Antonio society to display their means through architectural extravagance.

The importance of the San Antonio River to this section of the city has been somewhat altered through flood control measures enacted after the tragic inunda-

tion of 1921. At the foot of King William Street, there is a 1960s river channel. The control that has been exerted over the river tends to obscure the greatest endeavor of the mission system, the irrigation of fields by means of dams and aqueducts and *acequias*, or ditches. Fortunately, Espada Aqueduct survives as a splendid and romantic reminder of the prodigious energies of the Franciscan missionaries.

Wolfgang Host   Esto

96 NR
U.S. ARSENAL COMPLEX, from 1859
311 East Arsenal Street

An adjunct to the Quartermaster Depot
housed at the old Alamo buildings, this
arsenal was established in 1859 to supply
arms and ammunition to the U.S. Army's
frontier forts in Texas. Six main buildings of
limestone, including an officers' quarters
with Italianate details, were assembled in
the complex over several years. During the
two world wars, the San Antonio Arsenal
was a major supply depot for trans-shipment
of munitions. The H.E.B. grocery company
recently purchased part of the site and converted it to the firm's corporate headquarters
(see 95) with extensive renovation and
additions. The U.S. government still
utilizes the remaining buildings.

95 NR
H.E.B. COMPANY HEADQUARTERS,
1985
646 South Main Avenue
Hartman-Cox and Chumney/Urrutia

Rather than lodge its corporate headquarters in a high-rise tower, the H. E. Butt
Grocery Company purchased 11 acres of
the former U.S. Army Arsenal, which
occupied this site from 1859 until 1947, and
undertook adaptive reuse of two 19th-cen-
tury stone buildings and a series of imposing
industrial buildings constructed in 1916.
For H.E.B, the Washington, D.C., architects Hartman-Cox created a new, internally focused corporate campus. A former
warehouse became the River Building.
Enhanced with gabled second-story bays
and a central loggia, it contains the employees' dining rooms. The North Building, visible from East Durango Boulevard, is the
only completely new building in the complex. Housing the company's executive
offices, it was composed and detailed in a
stripped classical style corresponding to that
of the monumentally scaled South Building,
one of a pair of 400-foot long, 5-story
warehouses that back up to Arsenal Street.
Hartman-Cox's approach is consistently
undemonstrative, as the industrially
inspired classical detail and greenish-beige
stucco and blue-gray trim colors attest.
Chumney/Urrutia were interior architects;
James E. Keeter was landscape architect;
and Raiford Stripling & Associates of San
Augustine were consulting architects for
restoration of the Arsenal Magazine (1860)
and the Arsenal Stable (1874).

97 NR
COMMANDER'S HOUSE, circa 1883
647 South Main Avenue
Renovated, 1978
James (Bert) Whitaker

Dr. J.M. Devine built this imposing Italianate house of rusticated limestone on the outskirts of the city, across the river from King William Street. The tile roof further acknowledged a Mediterranean influence, and a wraparound double gallery served to make the house a pleasant retreat. The adjacent U.S. Arsenal, begun in 1860 and expanded over the years, eventually absorbed Devine's house, and it was made the arsenal commander's residence. Presently the house is operated by the San Antonio Department of Parks and Recreation and the San Antonio Junior Forum as a senior citizens' community center.

98
WESTMINSTER PRESBYTERIAN
CHURCH, 1948
1443 South St. Mary's Street
Henry Steinbomer

Steinbomer was not only one of the first architects to examine historic Texas buildings, he was one of the best at interpreting the subtleties of "regionalism" in new design. The stuccoed stone walls of the sanctuary manipulate the bright Central Texas sunlight with projecting entry-bay masses, deep-set fenestration, and textured surfaces. The campanile is massive, as if two facing buttresses were thrust above the roofline to support the bell. A utilitarian education wing, built in 1928, achieves sophistication through its 6-over-1 windows with sidelights, and its entry bays. The far entry is set deep beneath a scolloped arch, with a baroque *espadana* above.

99 NR
WRIGHT HOUSE, circa 1917
342 Wilkins Avenue
George Willis
Restored, 1981
DeLara-Almond

Willis studied under Frank Lloyd Wright and was associated in San Antonio with Atlee B. Ayres. Willis brought F.L. Wright's Midwestern residential style to San Antonio with this commission for (unrelated) client Lawrence Wright, who had sold the house by 1918. The low roof and wide eaves of the Prairie School are supported by tile-block walls finished with stucco. Painter Fred Donecker added a folk-art touch to the interior with murals and stenciling, accenting typical Craftsman-era interior woodwork. The house and decorative interior have been recently restored.

100
YTURRI-EDMUNDS COMPOUND,
1840
257 Yellowstone
Enlarged, 1860
Restored, 1961-70
Marvin Eichenrodt

Not far from the great mission church of Concepción, the Yturri-Edmunds Compound marks the rare survival of the sort of small farmstead that once was a prominent feature on the banks of the San Antonio River. Formerly part of the lands of Mission Concepción, the property was owned by the Yturri family and became the Edmunds property by virtue of a marriage in the 1870s. The principal structure is the house, a significant work and one of the few documented specimens of adobe construction in San Antonio. The adobe was formed using goat's hair mixed with stucco as a binding agent. While the site has been encroached upon by 20th-century industrialization, one can still acquire a sense of life here in the 1860s, especially with Mission Concepción so near.

THE SPANISH MISSIONS

Among the most impressive historical and architectural monuments in the U.S., the San Antonio missions (five, including the Alamo) were established by Spanish governors and missionaries during the period 1718-1731 as part of an effort to colonize Texas and civilize the Indians. Each four-to-five-acre compound was similar in plan, consisting of thick stone walls—with main gate and tower, and corner bastions—enclosing dwellings, workshops, stables, a granary, a convento or monastery, and the mission church, all arranged around a central court. Throughout the miniature township, the Indians cultivated agricultural plots irrigated by an acequia built to channel water from the nearby river. Of course the church itself received the most architectural attention, reflecting the Old-World craftsmanship of sculptors and artisans who took pride in their ornate forms delicately carved with embellishments of various derivations.

The missions have been reconstructed to varying degrees during a long history that has included some periods of neglect. In 1983, the Mission Parkway National Historic District was created by the National Park Service after years of planning and negotiation to link the four lower Spanish missions along a parkway. The NPS shares some administration of the sites with the Texas Parks and Wildlife Department and the local archdiocese of the Catholic church.

Mission Trail

101 NR
MISSION CONCEPCIÓN, 1731-55
(Nuestra Señora de la Purísima
Concepción de Acuña)
807 Mission Road at Mitchell
Restored, 1981
Ford, Powell & Carson

The walls of the mission compound have long-since vanished, and remaining auxiliary structures are partial ruins. But the church at Concepción (1755) is the most intact of all original structures at the San Antonio missions, and perhaps the most beautifully proportioned. The twin bell towers of light porous limestone were finished during the initial construction period. And neither the nave vault, known for its excellent acoustics, nor the crossing dome has ever collapsed. The exquisitely carved wood door and Plateresque detailing around portals, windows, and towers are characteristic of the sparse but expressive ornamentation the friars drew upon to provide cultural and spiritual enrichment in an otherwise primitive setting. Some faint traces of paint on the stuccoed facade remain to indicate the original colorful designs applied by local artisans—brilliant quatrefoils and squares of red, blue, orange and yellow. The church remains an active parish sanctuary, but all other structures and grounds are now administered by the National Park Service.

Mission Trail

102 NR
MISSION SAN JOSÉ, 1768-70
(San José y San Miguel de Aguayo)
6539 San Jose at Roosevelt
Reconstructed, 1928-36
Harvey P. Smith
Restored, 1984
Ford, Powell & Carson

Founded in 1720 and moved to its present site in 1740, San José had fallen into ruins by the early years of this century, despite its claim to some of the most beautiful carved-stone detail in the New World. Its dome and vault had collapsed and finally its bell tower crumbled to the ground. The San Antonio Conservation Society began its long record of preservation activities by restoring the mission granary in the 1920s. Rebuilding of the bell tower began in 1928 and, with the help of federal public works programs in the 1930s, the dome and vault were reconstructed of reinforced concrete. Other auxiliary structures, including the compound walls, were also restored and reconstructed during this period. The massive entry doors of the church are reproductions carved by Austin artisan Peter Mansbendel. Churrigueresque styling is reflected in the church's elaborate frontispiece, and in the sacristy's famous "Rosa's Window," believed to have been carved by Pedro Huizar. The church at San José is still an active sanctuary. The rest of the complex, administered by the Texas Parks and Wildlife Department and the National Park Service, affords visitors the best insight into what mission life was like in the 18th century.

Mission Trail

103 NR
ESPADA AQUEDUCT AND DAM,
Circa 1731-45
9044 Espada Road

The missions along the San Antonio River were ensured a constant flow of water for the inhabitants and their crops by systems of *acequias*, or irrigation canals. The Espada system, still flowing and considered the oldest such construction in the United States, begins at a limestone-rubble dam on the old river channel. It crosses Piedras Creek via an aqueduct built of limestone rubble, with a channel four feet wide and four feet deep. The aging system has been protected from the river's flood waters by new diversion canals.

104 NR
MISSION SAN JUAN, circa 1746-56
(San Juan Capistrano)
9101 Graf at Ashley
Restored, 1970 and 1980
Ford, Powell & Carson

Founded in 1731, along with Concepción and Espada, Mission San Juan was actually constructed between 1746 and 1756. A larger church was intended for the mission complex, but was never finished. Its foundations, along with those of the Indian quarters and other buildings, were unearthed during public works-sponsored investigations in the 1930s. The chapel, with its *espadaña*, or bell assembly, was rebuilt in the 1960s, along with the priest's quarters and other structures.

105 NR
MISSION ESPADA, 1731-45
(San Francisco de la Espada)
10040 Espada Road
Reconstructed, 1935
Harvey P. Smith
Restored, 1984
Ford, Powell & Carson

The timber-roofed chapel at Espada was built as an adjunct to a larger limestone church within a walled mission compound. Its *espadaña* is built of stuccoed rubble limestone with an unusual cut-stone entry frame. Restoration architects believe that the perimeter of this Mudéjar arch should be circular, and that early workmen fitted the pieces incorrectly.

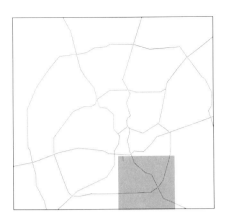

King William

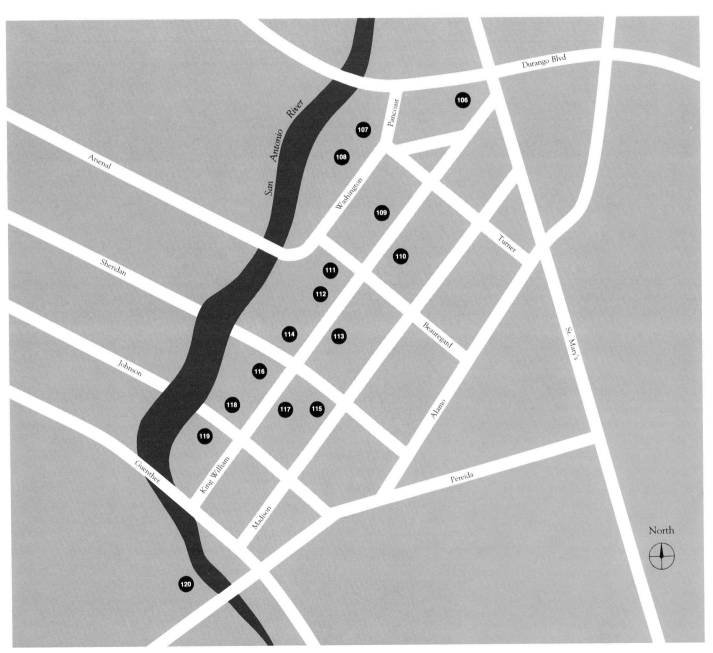

North

King William

Without question this is the city's most famous residential neighborhood, and deservedly so, containing a high concentration of late 19th- and early 20th-century homes in a variety of styles. The origins of the neighborhood date back to the 1860s, when Ernst Altgelt, a lawyer who had moved to San Antonio from Comfort, Texas, had three parallel avenues laid out along with five cross streets. The central avenue was named in honor of Kaiser Wilhelm I of Prussia, since Anglicized to King William. There is no better street in Texas on which to view the progress of post-Civil War domestic architecture, especially in terms of the development of that most American of house types, the suburban villa. The scale of the houses ranges from the compact Alex Sartor house at 217 King William, with its delightful detailing, to the flamboyant polychromed Romanesque of the George Kalteyer House at 425 King William. The 20th century is well represented by the large Colonial Revival houses for Thomas Flannery and Alexander Joske, located at 138 and 241 King William, respectively. The period of general neglect that began in the 1940s has been successfully arrested. King William resident Walter Mathis sparked the current interest in preservation of the neighborhood, resulting in a city historic district designation in 1967, and a very active neighborhood association.

106 NR
WULFF HOUSE, 1870
107 King William Street

By virtue of its siting, the Wulff House appears to have been built to serve as the gate lodge for the entrance to King William Street. The design of the house, perhaps more so than any other in the area, reflects the influence of the Italianate style as publicized by the books of Andrew Jackson Downing. The rough character of the exterior masonry would have pleased Downing, as would the asymmetrical character of the design. The significance of the arrangement of the interior rooms is revealed on the exterior by the location of the ornamental frame verandahs. Since 1975 the house has served as the headquarters of the San Antonio Conservation Society and is open to the public, although it is not set up as a house museum.

107 NR
OGE HOUSE, 1857
209 Washington Street
Remodeled, 1882
Alfred Giles

This house, which looks like it belongs on the outskirts of Charleston, is the product of a wholesale remodeling by Alfred Giles. The original structure, built in the late 1850's, probably resembled the nearby Blersch House at 213 Washington. The dominant columned verandahs, as well as the top floor of the present house, were all added by Giles for Louis Oge. The detailing of the front door and the Palladian opening onto the second-level verandah are exceptional, evoking a style of architecture that was alien to this city, at least in the 19th century.

King William

108 NR
BLERSCH HOUSE, 1860
213 Washington Street

With its riverside location, the Blersch House appears to pre-date the actual planning of the streets in the King William area. The scale of the house, along with its deep front verandah, suggests the influence of the Greek Revival style, although not in a strictly correct manner. While the King William District is perhaps best known for its large-scale residences, it does contain a number of small-scale houses of some importance and quality.

109 NR
SARTO HOUSE, 1881
217 King William Street
Alfred Giles

Although Alfred Giles is best known for larger commissions, such as the nearby Groos and Steves houses, he was also capable of creating delightful small-scale works like this house created for a jeweler who had emigrated from Germany. The detailing of the street front includes a handsome frame verandah sheltering five large wall openings that open onto it. The front wall is a conceit utilizing stucco modeled to imitate ashlar masonry with protruding mortar joints.

110 NR
ALTGELT HOUSE, 1878
226 King William Street

This simple two-story limestone-walled residence is of significance not so much for its architectural character but for the activities of its builder. Ernst Altgelt had arrived in San Antonio in 1866 from the small town of Comfort, which he had helped to establish some 15 years before. Altgelt was a surveyor, and it was he who was responsible for the platting of the main streets of this neighborhood. Altgelt's German and American sentiments are revealed by the naming of the central street for Kaiser Wilhelm I of Prussia, with American presidents Washington and Madison providing the names of the flanking streets. Unfortunately, Altgelt died before the house was finished.

King William

111 NR
STEVENS HOUSE, 1881
303 King William Street

The Stevens House provides another example of how the Italianate style was transformed from the specimens shown in Andrew Jackson Downing's books into a more localized style. The necessary asymmetrical character of the style is clearly displayed on the main facade, accented by the polygonal bay on the first floor. Because of its small width, the house looks like it could have been placed in a rowhouse streetscape in Philadelphia. The strong character of the exterior limestone masonry walls clearly labels it as a product of central Texas, even though the style is an import from the Northeast.

112 NR
HUMMEL HOUSE, 1884
309 King William Street

The *L*-plan two-story house is a significant 19th-century Texas house type, and the Hummel House is a good example executed in limestone masonry. The form of the house, as well as the detailing, is derivative of the widely popular Italianate style, which first began to make its presence felt in Texas in the 1870s. The use of two varieties of verandah brackets also reflects the style's tendency toward multiple decorative forms.

King William

113 NR
OPPENHEIMER HOUSE, 1901
316 King William Street

The rather stark detailing of this house marks it as a late example of the Romanesque Revival style. The majority of the exterior walls are of brick, with a minimum of carved stone details—the opposite of what would have been the case a decade earlier. Nevertheless, it is a significant addition to the streetscape, reflecting the continued desirability of the street into the early years of the 20th century.

114 NR
GROOS HOUSE, 1880
(Riverplace)
335 King William Street
Alfred Giles

Four years after Giles had designed the home of Edward Steves he received the commission to design the residence of the banker Carl Groos. While Giles simplified the character of the masonry on the Groos House, he increased the applied embellishments, most notably the cast-iron verandahs that shade the main elevation. The design is given a more picturesque appearance by virtue of the polygonal bay on the south side of the house, and the somewhat undersized cupola atop the roof. The house was extensively remodeled in 1984 by Ford, Powell & Carson.

King William

115 NR
CHABOT HOUSE, 1876
403 Madison Street

The contrast between the simplicity of the masonry work and the elaboration of the frame verandahs is what makes the Chabot House interesting. The stonework is at its best on the three-bay main block, with narrow mortar joints that become larger and less carefully worked on the recessed southern wing of the house. The detailing of the millwork is similarly handled, with paired columns on the main block, and single columns on the wing. The change in baluster designs on the two lesser verandahs suggests that the jigsaw-cut flat balusters may represent a somewhat later addition.

116 NR
NORTON-POLK-MATHIS HOUSE, 1876
401 King William Street
Additions, 1881

One of the more monumental houses in the King William area, the Norton-Polk-Mathis house represents two distinct building campaigns. Russel C. Norton, a hardware merchant, began the house, and the third-story tower and rear wing were added by Edward Polk. Although research has never connected an architect with the design of the house, the quality of the craftsmanship displayed on the limestone walls suggests that, at the very least, a master mason was employed in its construction. The ornamental fence surrounding the property combines limestone with cast- and wrought-iron in a fitting enclosure for so grand a residence.

King William

117 NR
ELLIS HOUSE, 1888
(West House)
422 King William Street

This three-story residence must be considered something of a hybrid, combining Second Empire and Italianate elements. The heavy character of the detailing of the masonry walls reflects the tradition of substantial brickwork that is so much a part of the area's architecture. The simplified French roof, ornamented with cast-iron cresting, serves to emphasize the massing of the house. The central focus of the design is the elaborately detailed entrance bay, whose cylindrical two-story porch is richly embellished with turned woodwork.

118 NR
KALTEYER HOUSE, 1892
425 King William Street
James Riely Gordon

Designed by the most celebrated of all 19th-century Texas architects, the Kalteyer house is perhaps the most architecturally significant structure on this noted street. Gordon, who is best known for his superb county courthouses in Texas, was also an excellent residential designer. This house, with its abundance of polychromed arches, reflects

Gordon's interest in the powerful masonry forms that are associated with the Romanesque Revival of the 1880s. Unfortunately, the great majority of Gordon's domestic work has long since been demolished, making this specimen all the more precious to the city.

King William

120 NR
GUENTHER HOUSE, 1860
205 East Guenther Street
Carl Guenther
Remodeled, 1917
Erhard Guenther

119 NR
STEVES HOMESTEAD, 1875
509 King William Street
Alfred Giles

With its large and heavily landscaped site, the Steves Homestead perhaps best represents the quality of life led by the families of wealthy San Antonio businessmen in the 1870s. The house is one of the earliest works of the English-born architect Alfred Giles, whose career had a profound influence on architecture in San Antonio. His client, Edward Steves, made his considerable fortune from his retail lumber business. The house reflects Giles's ability to combine elements of architecture both native and imported into a single design. For its day, this must be considered a rather restrained work, the mass of the house being confined to a single block with a service wing. Since 1952 it has been the property of the San Antonio Conservation Society, which operates it as a house museum. The interior was accurately restored on the basis of a large number of 19th-century photographs of the house that survived in the possession of Edward Steves's descendants. Also of note, although it no longer serves its original function, is the one-story building toward the river side of the property. Constructed around 1900 by Edward Steves's widow, it housed a covered swimming pool that was filled from an artesian well on the grounds.

Situated on what is surely the most romantic site in the neighborhood, overlooking the San Antonio River, the Guenther House is more a product of this century than of the 19th. The only section of Carl Hilmar Guenther's stone house still recognizable on the exterior is the one-story block that projects toward the river. His son Erhard was responsible for what amounts to a wholesale remodeling and rebuilding of the house around 1917. Externally, this work can be seen in the form of the three-story main block, with its green-tile roof and side verandah. The house, with its remarkable interiors and third-floor dance hall, is undergoing restoration by Pioneer Flour Mills.

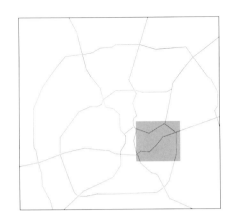

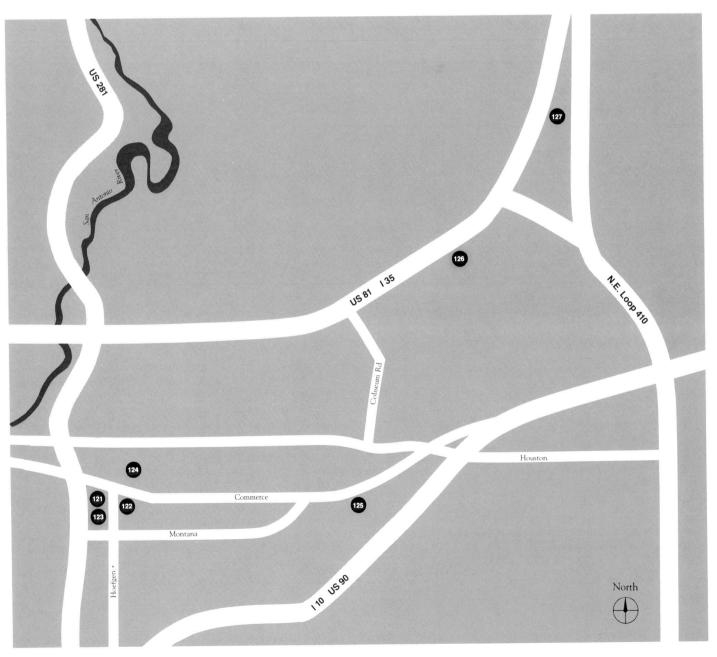

US 281

San Antonio River

US 81   I 35

Coliseum Rd

N.E. Loop 410

127

126

Houston

124

121

122

125

Commerce

123

Montana

Hoefgen

I 10   US 90

North

East

Severed from the city center by the inter-state highway, east San Antonio is now a world unto itself. But a visit to St. Paul Square suggests an earlier era when the east side supported commercial activity of major importance to the city. The major east-side force was the Southern Pacific Railroad line, still represented by its depot building of 1902. Curiously, the other major public work on the east side was the large city cemetery located to the south and east of the railroad's depot and yards.

By the turn of the century the city's trend toward northward growth was already estab-lished, but some significant residential con-struction did occur on the east side. Homes in the area surrounding Lockwood Park, known as the Dignowity Hill neighbor-hood, were featured in early 20th-century illustrated booklets touting the city's highly attractive quality of life.

In more recent times, the focus of archi-tectural and commercial development has been the interstate loop around the city. The best of this roadside architecture, typi-cally designed to be experienced at 55 miles per hour, includes the Pace Foods complex and the high-tech Muzak Systems office.

121 ★ NR
ST. PAUL SQUARE,
Circa 1905
1100 Block, East Commerce Street
Rehabilitated, 1979
Ford, Powell & Carson and
    Jordan & McCowan
SOUTH BLOCK, 1982 ★
Larry O'Neill & Andrew Perez with
    Joe Stubblefield

San Antonio never built a union passenger
station, and thus the early satellite commercial centers that grew up around its three
major rail depots thrived until after World
War II. The Southern Pacific Railroad
established its terminal east of the city
center, and these adjacent two- and three-
story brick businesses sprouted nearby along
East Commerce Street. Dilapidated and
separated from downtown in recent years by
the raised grade of Interstate 37, the group-
ing was the focus of a 1979 redevelopment
project centering on the depot and new offices for Ford, Powell & Carson. Restored
fronts, covered rear walkways, and over-
head handicap access unifies the facing
commercial rows. Cohesiveness of the complex is further enhanced by street furniture
and pleasant outdoor courts.

123
HEIMANN BUILDING, circa 1906
(Steves and Sons)
122 Heimann Street
Atlee B. Ayres
Rehabilitated, 1985

122 NR
SOUTHERN PACIFIC PASSENGER
    DEPOT, 1903
1174 East Commerce Street
D.J. Patterson, John D. Isaacs
Renovated 1981-84

Southwestern railroads were among the first clients to proliferate Mission and Spanish Colonial Revival styles. Patterson and Isaacs—architect and engineer, respectively—were employed by the Southern Pacific Railroad in its San Francisco offices when they transferred a growing California trend to San Antonio with this depot. The brick structure's exterior is stuccoed and highlighted with cast-stone details. The interior is strictly Beaux-Arts, with plaster-cast garlands and a sweeping barrel vault illuminated by art-glass windows and skylight. Years of alterations were removed in the recent renovation, which left the interior reflecting a c. 1940 configuration.

This Mission Revival building is an important element of the St. Paul Square Historic District. Its corner tower with open belvedere reflects the similarly styled Southern Pacific Passenger Depot across the street. Last used as a hotel during HemisFair in 1968, the building was abandoned and almost lost to a gutting fire in 1982, but has been restored as the corporate offices of Steves and Sons. It has a stuccoed finish, highlighted by exposed brick structural elements. The tower's restored roof is actually pressed tin simulating tile—an exact copy of the original roof detail.

125 ★
SECOND BAPTIST CHURCH, 1968
3310 East Commerce Street
Norcel Haywood and
    Ford, Powell & Carson

124
SAMSCO BUILDING, circa 1880, 1912
(G.J. Sutton State Office Building)
321 North Center Street
Rehabilitated, 1982
Ford, Powell & Carson

This adaptive-use state office complex was
once part of a larger industrial complex
developed from the 1880s. San Antonio
Machine and Supply Company
(SAMSCO) was a machine shop and foun-
dry that moved to existing brick buildings
here in 1904. Brick additions were made
c. 1906 and in 1912. The firm flourished
before World War I, manufacturing
windmills and equipment for the cattle
industry in the southwestern U.S. and
northern Mexico. A six-story addition of

concrete frame and brick curtain wall was
built c.1960 on the firm's north end.
SAMSCO sold the complex in 1965 and
the State of Texas acquired the buildings in
1975, adapting them to office use.

Counter-thrust shed roofs covered with
standing-seam metal, walls of variegated
tan brick ornamented with decorative
bonding patterns, and the picturesque juxtaposition of building masses around a central atrium are hallmarks of O'Neil Ford's
architectural production during the 1960s.
Here, these properties allow the church
complex to be centered around the protected garden court while still permitting it
to project distinctive images toward the
street (a commercial strip)—and the rear
parking lot.

Rick Gardner

126 ★
PACE FOODS, 1983
3750 North Pan Am Expressway
Ford, Powell & Carson

A modest, economical, and carefully composed food production plant and administrative office building, Pace Foods represents Chris Carson's effort to derive a southwestern regional architecture without resorting to kitsch styling. Constructed of concrete tilt-wall panels, it is finished externally in stucco; red metal window frames provide a dash of color. The glazed administrative area, facing the freeway, is set off behind a walled garden forecourt. The production zone is skylit and naturally ventilated.

127
MUZAK SYSTEMS, 1983
4242 North Pan Am Expressway
Larry O'Neill & Andrew Perez

Situated on a low rise and inflected toward the freeway, this small office and warehouse building is bold-faced and ambiguously scaled. Inset within its gridded brown clay-tile facade is a second grid of glass-block apertures, admitting light to offices while filtering out traffic noise. The Muzak pylon bearing a satellite microwave dish, the stepped projecting bay opposite it, and the up-turned steel space frame that spans between them bracket an imposing entrance to the modest building behind.

80

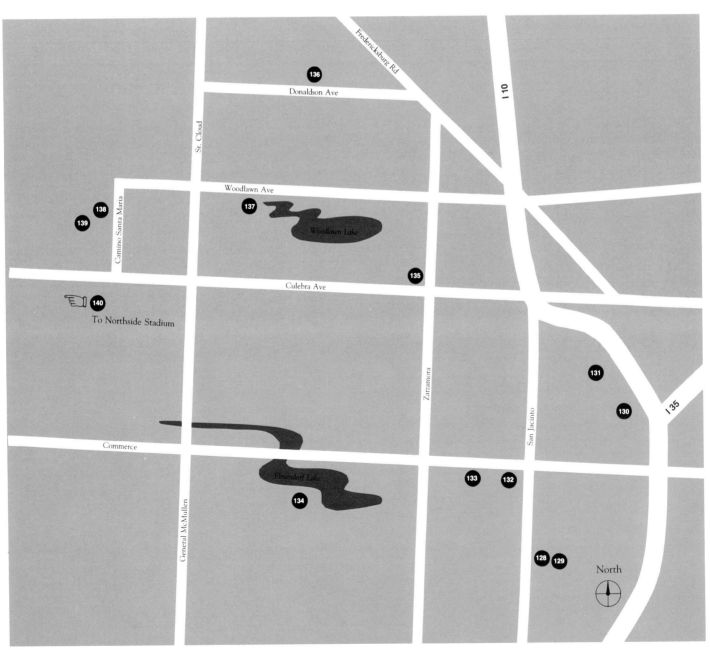

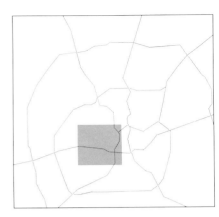

West

Despite west San Antonio's proximity to Main and Military plazas, the city's 19th-century commercial and governmental core, the area was slow to develop both residentially and commercially. An 1886 bird's-eye-view map of the city indicates that this area still was quite sparsely populated, the tracks of the International and Great Northern Railroad appearing as an isolated improvement.

A period of growth between 1890 and 1910 followed the platting of the Prospect Hill addition, which by the turn of the century housed numerous middle-class residents. Their cottage residences stood alongside public works such as the Prospect Hill Missionary Baptist Church of 1911.

The area's character changed forever with the Mexican Revolution of 1910. This cataclysmic event, which brought about near-total anarchy in Mexico, forced a massive immigration of Mexican nationals into Texas, particularly San Antonio. Many of the immigrants settled near Guadal·ipe Avenue, and the street soon became lined with small family-run businesses that serviced the new Hispanic community. The area was largely developed by resident property owners, with little absentee landlord ownership of the housing stock.

By the late 1930s, efforts to upgrade the neighborhood's housing included the construction of small-scale public housing units, which fortunately maintained the neighborhood's character. In recent years the Hispanic community has reinvigorated the neighborhood with Plaza Guadalupe and a highly imaginative reuse of the old Guadalupe Theater—two of the city's best recent works of architecture.

The West Side suburbs also house two Catholic institutions: Our Lady of the Lake University and St. Mary's University, both with major buildings by James Wahrenberger. Despite the city's continued westward growth, the settings of both schools still reflect something of their original pastoral feel.

129
GUADALUPE THEATER, 1941
(Guadalupe Cultural Arts Center)
1300 Guadalupe Street
Remodeled, 1984
Reyna-Caragonne

128 ★
PLAZA GUADALUPE, 1984
1300 Block, Guadalupe Street
Reyna-Caragonne

The plaza is a brilliant urban design scheme that fuses baroque planning and extroverted architectural imagery with the properties of southwestern regionalism. Organized along a mid-block axis focused on the parroquia of Nuestra Senora de Guadalupe (1921, Leo M. J. Dielmann) are a sequence of open-air spaces. Light modulating screen walls and pergolas, combined with vivid patterns and colors, imbue this public square with a joyous, festive atmosphere. Reyna-Caragonne has acknowledged the cultural context of the neighborhood without resorting to folkloric cliches. Subsequent phases of development will include a clinic and a public bazaar. At Guadalupe and Brazos is the former Progreso Theater (1941), now rehabilitated as the Guadalupe Theater (see #129).

Reyna Caragonne's exuberant rehabilitation of a former neighborhood vaudeville and movie theater to accommodate live performances, film, and community social events involved judicious conservation of existing external details and complete interior reconstruction. As at the adjacent Plaza Guadalupe (of which this a component), the neighborhood vocabulary of glazed-tile finishes and glass block has been adopted and intensified with wit and intelligence. Public spaces inside are ceremonious and festive.

130
KQXT-FM, 1981
1115 West Martin Street
Swanson Hiester Wilson Claycomb and
    Saldana, Williams & Schubert

Sharply contoured profiling, advancing and receding masses, and shaped screen walls imbue this complex of radio broadcast studios and offices with a forceful public aspect while enabling it to remain insulated from external noise and visual interference. Finished entirely in textured concrete masonry units—a signature material of SHWC designer William L. Wadley—the complex is linked visually to nearby downtown buildings by its buff color. This is the one architecturally distinguished building in a former inner-city neighborhood drastically suburbanized by urban renewal.

131
CHAPEL OF MIRACLES, circa 1870s
113 Ruiz Street

Stranded incongruously between a freeway frontage road and a series of garden apartment complexes are this tiny devotional chapel, built as a pious work by Don Juan Ximenes and maintained as such by his decendants, and the adjacent Ximenes House. The chapel contains an eight-foot-high wooden Spanish crucifix which, according to tradition, originally hung in the church of Mission San Antonio de Valero, and to which miraculous restorative power is attributed. The present building, of plastered stone construction, probably dates from the 1870s, but its current appearance stems from a remodeling in 1946. Urban renewal is responsible for alienating the Chapel of the Miracles and the Ximenes House from their original neighborhood setting.

132
OLD PROSPECT HILL BAPTIST
CHURCH, 1911
1601 Buena Vista
Henry J. Harker, Little Rock, Ark.
Rehabilitated, 1984
John Bratton & Ernest Breig

This structure has undergone one of the most dramatic conversions of any building in San Antonio. Designed by the Little Rock, Arkansas, architect Henry J. Harker, the structure housed a large Baptist congregation that disbanded in 1965. The church, which featured a prominent low dome and monumental round-arched window bays, was gutted by fire in 1980. The rehabilitation of the building as apartments for the elderly required the installation of five lift slabs within the original masonry walls. While the domed interior of the church could not be restored, an external dome structure was installed in an effort to recreate the building's original massing.

133 ★
MEXICAN-AMERICAN UNITY
COUNCIL, 1912
2300 West Commerce Street
Leo M. J. Dielmann
Alterations and additions, 1930
Carl V. Seutter
Rehabilitation, 1977
Larry O'Neill & Andrew Perez

Dielmann's elementary school for the west
side neighborhood of Prospect Hill is monumentally scaled and detailed with abstract,
New French classical ornament. These
attributes endow it with a sense of presence
that serves it well in its current status as a
community center. O'Neill & Perez
installed new glazing but did not otherwise
alter the exteriors. The grounds have been
enclosed and landscaped to serve the center
as a small park.

134
OUR LADY OF THE LAKE
UNIVERSITY, 1900-1924
411 Southwest 24th Street
James Wahrenberger (Main Building, St.
    Ann's Hall, Moye Hall)
Leo M. J. Dielmann (Conventual Chapel,
    Providence Hall, Library)

The splendid collection of buildings that
constitutes Our Lady of the Lake would be
noteworthy anywhere in San Antonio, but
here, on the city's west side, they are a stag-
gering presence. The physical scale of the
complex makes it visible from far out on
West Commerce, and the site, adjacent to
Elmendorf Lake, is wonderfully romantic.
Erected for the Sisters of Divine Provid-
ence, an order founded in France, the archi-

tectural character of the complex is suitably
Gallic, although the interior of the Conventual Chapel is decidedly English Gothic
in feeling. Wahrenberger's work here is typical of his somewhat aggressive manner,
with a sizable quota of spiky towers, some of
which are crenelated. While Dielmann
arrived late on the scene, he was given the
choice commission for the centerpiece of
the school, the magnificent Conventual
Chapel. Its spire soars 193 feet above the
ground, and its interior boasts a fine collection of stained glass from the Munich artist
Emil Frei. Both of the architects for Our
Lady of the Lake were favorites of the Catholic community in San Antonio, and it is
altogether fitting that some of their best
work should stand side by side on this
campus.

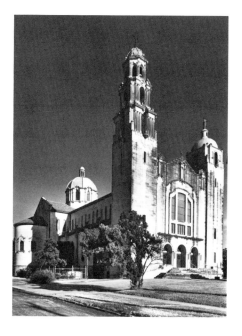

135
SHRINE OF THE LITTLE FLOWER, 1931
906 West Kentucky Street
C.L. Monnot, Oklahoma City

The Discalced Carmelite Fathers, an order
within the Roman Catholic Church, con-
ducted a national campaign after 1927 to
fund their shrine in San Antonio. The
church structure consists of a delicate steel
nave framework, surrounded by masonry
walls clad with Indiana limestone. Spanish
Renaissance details have been applied spar-
ingly on the edifice, which relies largely on
its mass for domination of the neighborhood. One front tower rises 116 feet, and
the other, at 72 feet, is topped by a bronze
statue of St. Therese—the Little Flower.
Art glass windows and elaborate statuary
enliven the cross-vaulted interior.

136 NR
THOMAS JEFFERSON HIGH SCHOOL,
1932
723 Donaldson Avenue
Adams & Adams
East Wing and Shop, 1963
Phelps & Simmons

LIFE magazine focused national attention
on this rambling, two- and three-story complex with an article in the 1930s on its student life. A four-story domed tower anchors
the asymmetrical composition. Spanish
Colonial Revival detailing in cast stone
reaches an apex with the elaborate Baroque

main entry bay. Elsewhere, subtle pauses
between detailing are accomplished with
brick veneer. Student union and gym-
nasium additions have been built, and
aluminum windows were installed in 1978.

137
ASSUMPTION SEMINARY CHAPEL,
1974
2600 West Woodlawn Avenue
Ford, Powell & Carson

The chapel is situated within high, window-
less walls of *opus incertum* construction—
bracketed on two sides by a lower concrete-
walled adjunct containing the narthex and
side chapels. It is sheltered beneath a deeply
coffered, two-way structural canopy of wood
carried on twin ranks of free-standing concrete columns. Boone Powell admitted natural light through a monitor between the
canopy and the east wall, throwing into
relief the screened perimeter of the chapel
sanctuary. Lynn Ford executed the abundant decorative woodwork in the chapel
and narthex; liturgical instruments and furniture complement the architecture.

138
ST. MARY'S UNIVERSITY
ADMINISTRATION BUILDING, 1894
1 Camino Santa Maria
James Wahrenberger

Originally St. Louis College, the Main
Building at St. Mary's was built on a prom-
ontory overlooking the distant suburb of
West End Heights to house boarding students from St. Mary's School, then downtown. The building displays Wahrenberger's
characteristic High Victorian composi-
tional traits: subdivision into symmetrical
groups of threes, horizontality broken by
central vertical accents, and "constructive"
brick ornament. Here, however, Wahrenberger dispensed with the color contrasts
so familiar in his other buildings. As a
result, the cream-colored fabric appears
subdued, despite the lively detail. Unfortunately, the emphatic frontality of the college building has discouraged subsequent
campus architects from attempting to inte-
grate new construction with it, rendering
the main building literally and figuratively
peripheral to the interior of the campus.

140 ★
PAUL TAYLOR FIELD HOUSE, 1975
Culebra Road and N.W. Loop 410
Marmon & Mok Associates

139
SARITA KENEDY EAST LAW
LIBRARY, 1984
St. Mary's University
Jones & Kell

Not since the construction of Wahrenberger's main building has St. Mary's experienced this calibre of architectural production. The law library is a witty exposition of unorthodox detail, an architectural send-up of the lugubrious arch-o-mania that gripped St. Mary's in the middle 1960s. Contextuality, solar orientation, and the uses of internal spaces are addressed in the transformation of the curtain wall, where John H. Kell, Jr., with a tense equivocation, arouses, then subverts, conventional expectations about the nature and roles of materials. In contrast, the interiors of the library are serene and tranquil, generously proportioned, and subtly detailed. The public spaces afford sweeping views across the as-yet undeveloped western and southern portions of the campus.

Built in two phases to serve the Northside Independent School District, the field house is an expressively shaped sports arena of reinforced concrete construction faced with precast concrete panels. The projecting ends, which give the building its distinctive profile, are the cantilevered upper tiers of two banks of seating that confront each other across the depressed basketball court.

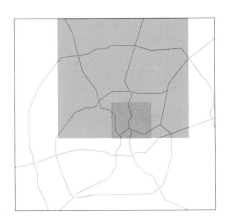

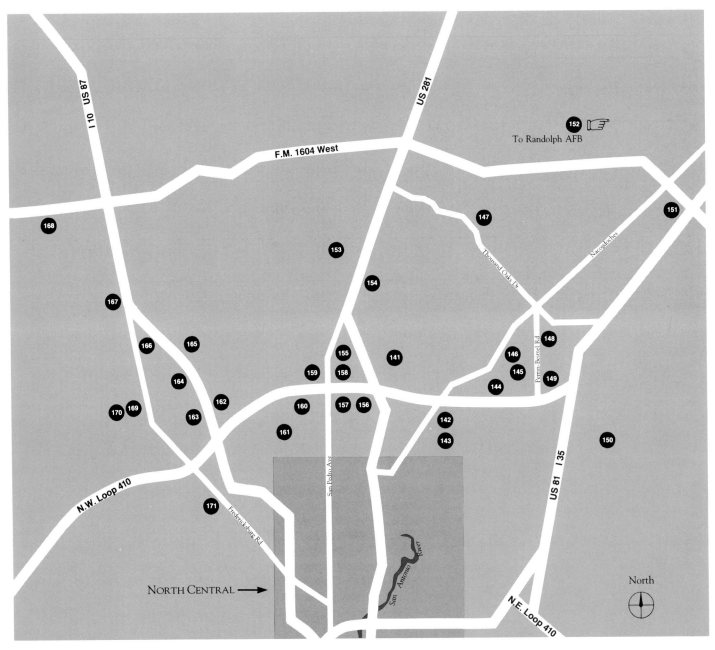

US 87

I 10

US 281

152 👉
To Randolph AFB

F.M. 1604 West

147

151

168

Thousand Oaks Dr.

Nacogdoches

153

154

167

148

Perrin-Beitel Rd.

166

165

146

141

155

145

164

159

158

144

149

162

170 **169**

160

157 **156**

163

161

142

143

150

US 81 I 35

N.W. Loop 410

San Pedro Ave.

Fredericksburg Rd.

171

San Antonio River

North

NORTH CENTRAL →

N.E. Loop 410

North

Contrary to its romantic and popular image, modern-day San Antonio is of course more a product of this century than of the 18th or 19th, and nowhere is this more evident than in the architecture of north San Antonio. As the city grew dramatically in population from the 1890s through the 1930s, making San Antonio the largest city in Texas, local publicists championed the quality of life in Tobin Hill and its neighbor to the north, Laurel Heights. Both suburbs are liberally sprinkled with the work of the city's best architects, with Kings Highway representing the apogee of the boom period between the World Wars.

The regular grid pattern of Tobin Hill and Laurel Heights was decisively broken by the second generation of suburbs, which began when the Alamo Heights Land and Improvement Company purchased a large tract in 1893. Alamo Heights became the first true garden suburb in Texas, relying on curvilinear streets to provide variety of setting to its residents. The construction of a streetcar line along Broadway was a major boost to this development. On the heels of Alamo Heights came Olmos Park, the most topographically interesting real estate in the area, and Terrell Hills, a tract of flatter land suitable for massive suburban estates. While these three suburbs tended to cater to upper-income groups, other tracts such as Beacon Hill and Los Angeles Heights became the domain of the small-scale bungalow. North San Antonio also houses nonresidential work of major significance, including the campus of Trinity University, begun in 1949.

Recent years have seen a second great wave of northward development, as Interstate Loop 410 has spawned what is tantamount to a second city along its path. Growth beyond the loop in the last 20 years has included a new branch of the University of Texas at San Antonio, begun in the 1970s. Today San Antonio is the tenth largest city in the United States, and its northward growth now presses to the limits of Bexar County itself.

142
NORTH FROST BANK BUILDING,
1981
1250 N.E. Loop 410
Rehler Vaughn Beaty & Koone

141 ★
SAN ANTONIO INTERNATIONAL
AIRPORT, TERMINAL ONE, 1984
139 Airport Boulevard
Heery/Marmon Mok/Simpson

The first stage of a four-phase program to replace the 1952 terminal building (Atlee B. and Robert M. Ayres) is an artful, ingenious, and exuberant work of architecture. Terry Sargent, chief designer for the Atlanta architects Heery and Heery, working with The Marmon Mok Partnership and W.E. Simpson Company, combined the precision of industrial construction and environmental technology with a spirited acknowledgment of San Antonio's architectural character. The terminal's checkered pink concrete masonry units and silvery aluminum banding, exposed tubular steel trusses, and lightweight acrylic, plastic, and perforated steel vaults produce brilliant contrasts of texture and color. The vaults, which imbue the main concourse level with a strong sense of spatial definition, admit filtered daylight through transverse ribbed slots. Even the 1,300-car parking garage is surfaced with Adoquin stone. Included in the first phase is the central mechanical plant, wittily pressed into service as a sculptural set piece and fountain. Heery and Heery were responsible for graphic and interior design and Marmon, Mok & Green for landscape architecture.

Knife-edged profiling, a sloped-glass lobby roof, and a neutral, gridded sheath of silver reflective glass imbue this 11-story office building with its image. A deep, horizontal shadow line between the tenth and eleventh floors implies a distinction between cap and shaft.

143
KELL HOUSE, 1972
2635 Brookhurst Drive
John H. Kell, Jr.

For a heavily wooded site verging on a shallow ravine at the corner of Brookhurst Drive and Cave Lane, John H. Kell, Jr. designed this stepped-level, double-faced house with a flat roof. A steel-framed, glazed pavilion containing the major living rooms projects from the rear of a cubic, brick-faced block, its glazing compacted into gridded metal bays. This makes for a sensuous, provocative juxtaposition of contrasting vocabularies, which Kell developed into a brash new architectural language in subsequent work.

144 ★
LOS PATIOS GARDEN CENTER, 1971
2015 N.E. Loop 410
Frank D. Welch
Gazebo and Hacienda, 1973 and 1977
Frank Welch Associates and Carrington,
    Weems & Associates

Notwithstanding its proximity to Loop 410, this specialty shopping center is set on a quiet, wooded, 33-acre estate along Salado Creek. Welch's buildings are purposefully understated. Small-scaled, shed-roofed, and stucco-faced, they are connected by pergolas, galleries, and landscaped courts, discretely inserted amidst the trees. The Gallery, the first and most carefully detailed building, is a combination house-and-store which incorporates a cast-stone Spanish-style portal salvaged from the demolished MK&T Railway Passenger Station (1915, Frederick J. Sterner). Ambiance, not the domination of architecture, is what was aimed for here; Los Patios is charming without being contrived.

Rick Gardner

145
EPISCOPAL CHURCH OF THE
RECONCILIATION, 1974
8900 Starcrest Drive
Ford, Powell & Carson

The liturgical centrality of the Eucharist
prompted both the square planning and
pyramidal massing of this small suburban
church, which occupies its flat, wooded site
with dignity and authority. The outer walls,
laid up in wide courses of salvaged limestone, are indented on three sides to provide
deep-set, enclosed garden bays, screened
from the outside by wooden slats. The high,
copper-clad lantern, rising above the central worship space, recalls in its shape the
vernacular buildings of the central Texas
countryside.

146
SAINT MARY'S HALL, 1968
9401 Starcrest Drive
Ford, Powell & Carson and Bartlett
    Cocke & Associates

A small, established private school for girls
set on a large, wooded tract, Saint Mary's
Hall represents Ford at his best. Clois-
tered passageways, some of arched masonry
construction, others of cedar post-and-
beam construction, ring a series of garden
courts to join the compactly clustered,
domestically scaled campus buildings. The
low-pitched, standing-seam metal roofs,
punctuated by clerestory bands or upthrust
sheds; simple but carefully articulated wood
joinery; and walls of dun-colored Mexican

brick are the stuff of Ford's regionalist
vocabulary. These properties allow the
architecture to merge with the cultivated
landscape and achieve the paradoxical goal
of romantic regionalism: that dream of tranquil timelessness that seeks to evade history
in order to become nature.

147 ★
PLAZA AT THOUSAND OAKS, 1984
2845 Thousand Oaks Drive
Riehm Owensby Guzman

Punctuated by pyramidally roofed tower
bays, this 48,000-square-foot office and
retail center frames a motor court and
pedestrian concourse. Plantings and fountains are allied with variations in massing,
materials, and colors to create a sense of
identity.

148 ★
UNITED STATES POSTAL SERVICE
GENERAL MAIL FACILITY, 1977
10410 Perrin Beitel Road
The Marmon Mok Partnership and
    Phelps Simmons Garza

Combined in this low-set, long-spread,
300,000-square-foot building are a post
office, regional mail-handling operations,
and a vehicle maintenance garage. The
horizontality of the building effectively
counters the gently rolling landscape in
which it is set. Glazing is recessed in deep
slots along the west elevation, providing
dark wells of shadow that underscore the
building's horizontal expanse. The projecting vertical bay denotes the front door of
the post office. A metal-panel wall system
cladding the steel-frame structure contrib-
utes to the building's quiet, imperturbable
look.

149 ★
BARTLETT COCKE JR.
CONSTRUCTION CO. OFFICES, 1982
4359 Industrial Center
JonesKell Architects

Built in an era when the surrounding acres
were rural farmland, this wooden frame
farmhouse in recent years found itself an
anachronism among industries along Loop
410. The house was converted to offices for
a local construction company, and in 1982
a 5,000-square-foot addition was completed
adjacent to the renovated residence. The
addition reflects its neighbor in scale and
calm response to established pecan trees;
red brick walls were inspired by the brick
chimneys of the farmhouse. Other walls of
glass blocks diffuse sunlight and views of
surrounding industries.

150 ★
GECU PROTOTYPE, 1980
8047 Midcrown Street
Chumney, Jones & Kell

Strategically located at a bend in a suburban commercial thoroughfare, this sleek,
elegantly detailed pavilion of bronze-tinted
glass walls— poised beneath a hovering roof
plane of white concrete and sunk behind
grass berms—stands in marked contrast to
its cluttered surroundings. Behind the
minimalist pavilion, drive-in stations are
grouped under a steel space-frame canopy.

151 ★
MORTON HOUSE, 1982
12590 Judson Road
Frank D. Welch

"Regional" architecture in Texas can be
many things, but it traditionally represents
a local response to climate with the best
materials available. Rough stone walls are
the sturdiest offering of the immediate vic-
inity, and sheet-metal roofs reflect an early
adoption of imported materials. Living
space in this contemporary residence is
efficiently managed with three gabled pavilions, linked by wraparound galleries and
accented by tall chimney stacks. The
ensemble effect is more akin to frontier fort
complexes than European immigrant structures of the region.

152
RANDOLPH AIR FORCE BASE
ADMINISTRATIVE BUILDING, 1931
(Taj Mahal)
Randolph Air Force Base
Atlee B. & Robert M. Ayres

Nicknamed the Taj Mahal by the airmen
who have trained here, the shining-white
structure still looms over the installation.
Truly multipurpose, the building contains a
1200-seat theater in its rear wing, and a
500,000- gallon water tank in the tower.
The blue- and-gold chevron-patterned
dome is derived from a number of mid-19th
century Mexican churches, the most notable being the Pociti Chapel in Mexico City.
The blind tracery of the tower shaft has its
roots in the architecture of Moorish Spain.

154
SKYPORT OFFICE PLAZA, 1981
100 Sandau Road
Sam Briggs

A stepped-plan configuration, cylindrical turrets, and unstinting use of reflective glass block render this three-story speculative office building a dazzling spectacle.

153 ★
HARVEY SCULPTURE STUDIO, 1983
411 West Rhapsody Street
Jones & Kell

This 1,500-square-foot studio and gallery for the fabrication and display of steel sculpture, located along a commercial strip thoroughfare, is an extraordinary building. John Kell, Jr., used expedient methods and materials (pre-engineered steel framing, an infill of red clay tile units, and metal roofing and doors) to achieve spectacular effects. Even the painting of exposed steel results in kaleidoscopic profusion. The principal interior spaces overlook a small garden on the downhill side of the site.

156 ★
CENTURY CENTER, 1973
84 N.E. Loop 410
Neuhaus + Taylor, Houston

Century Center's long, low shape was determined by then-current height-and-setback restrictions due to its proximity to the airport. One of the first speculative office buildings to be constructed along the Loop, it also was the first building in the city to be surfaced entirely in gold reflective glass. Neuhaus + Taylor's designer, Elmo Valdes, inserted an air-conditioned garden court beneath the tilted plane of the front elevation.

155
MAC 37 OFFICE BUILDING, 1983
10227 McAllister Freeway
Lance, Larcade & Bechtol

This small, two-story speculative office building faces the freeway with a reflective glass plane split down the middle and splayed inward toward an open-air circulation spine and courtyard. A vaulted canopy protecting the spine marks the entranceway to the building while acknowledging the sectional *leitmotiv* of the airport terminal nearby.

157
MERCANTILE BANK BUILDING, 1981
40 N.E. Loop 410
Skidmore, Owings & Merrill, Houston

This six-story, 220,000-square-foot bank and office building acknowledges its location at the intersection of the Loop and a major arterial street by the curvature of its main elevation, which cuts into the building above a three-story, glazed banking hall. SOM-Houston's designer, Richard Keating, combined light-toned granite-clad spandrels, reflective window glass, and metallic gray mullions in this sleek, understated composition.

158
LA MANSION DEL NORTE
COURTYARD, 1978
37 N.E. Loop 410
Harwood K. Smith & Partners, Dallas

The source of inspiration for this ersatz Mexican *convento* was Wallace B. Thomas's La Mansion del Rio on the River Walk. Like it, the five-story, 306-room La Mansion del Norte contains a landscaped central patio ringed with tiers of precast concrete columns. Designed by the landscape architect James Keeter, the patio garden, with its giant stone fountain and beds of tropical plantings, lends a note of substance to this freeway fantasy. The freestanding, open-cage elevator on the north side of the patio functions both as sculpture and as transportation.

159 ★
SASA CENTER, 1980
601 N. W. Loop 410
Hellmuth, Obata & Kassabaum, Dallas

The serrated profile of this nine-story, 240,000-square-foot corporate headquarters for the San Antonio Savings Association by HOK-Dallas rises dramatically at the crest of a small hill above the intersection of the Loop and San Pedro. Continuous spandrels surfaced with Texas Cordova limestone shield recessed horizontal ribbon windows. Terraces are developed on the south and east sides of the building above setback levels; there the spandrels harbor planting troughs.

160 ★
GPM HOME OFFICE BUILDING AND
SOUTH TOWER, 1969 and 1972
800 N.W. Loop 410
Bartlett Cocke & Associates

This pair of seven-story office buildings is
set on a landscaped podium above screened
and covered parking. The office buildings
are of reinforced concrete construction.
Dark tinted glass walls, constituting one of
the first uses of double-pane glass in San
Antonio, are carefully shaded by precast
perforated wall panels.

161
DUKES HOUSE, 1961
404 Travertine Drive
William H. Dukes

Set on a sloping site, this flat-roofed Modernist pavilion rides out over the landscape
on brick piers, a scheme consistent with the
interest of Dukes' colleague, Jack Peterson,
in conspicuous structural display. Toward
the street, the house exhibits a rhythmically
divided wall plane of cement asbestos panels
and redwood battens. Toward the west and
south, however, there is extensive glazing,
protected by the overhanging roof plane,
which is carried on a series of turned wooden
struts that fan out from the caps of the brick
piers.

162 ★
ST. ANDREW PRESBYTERIAN
CHURCH, 1963
8231 Callaghan Road
O'Neil Ford and Howard Wong

The influence of architect Louis I. Kahn on
American architecture in the 1960s is evident in this suburban church. It is square in
plan, braced by low corner buttresses, and
organized internally on diagonally rotated
cross-axes. The cubic lantern at the apex of
the pyramidal, wood-shingled roof admits
daylight at the center of the worship space.
Bands of corbelled indentations along the
tan brick walls, and Ford's familiar light
fixture fabrications are the only concessions
to ornament in this austere but unintimidat-
ing building. A low administration and
assembly wing adjoins the church on the
west.

164
SOUTHWEST AIRLINES
RESERVATION CENTER, 1981
3635 Medical Drive
Morris & McDonald

165
CANAVAN CENTER, 1970-1977
8647 Wurzbach Road
Ken Bentley & Associates

163 ★
ONE FORUM OFFICE BUILDING, 1983
(Tenneco Office Building)
800 I.H. 10 West
Hellmuth, Obata & Kassabaum, Dallas

A refined essay in precast concrete constructivist design, this three-story office block
wrapped around a 16-story tower is notable
for its ebullient rose color, intensified with
rose-colored reflective glass and a dramatic
stepped-back massing profile. Seen from the
west, across a valley full of condominiums,
the Forum rises authoritatively out of the
crest of Horizon Hill.

This low corporate office building is carefully adjusted to its rolling site. Battered
buttresses rhythmically divide the exterior
wall surfaces into a series of bays faced with
bronze tinted glass or light brown brick. A
deep concrete fascia features a running band
of sunk panels. Corporate graphics are cast-
in-place next to the main entrance.

In the best San Antonio tradition of Modernist regionalism, this complex of medical
professional offices, built over a period of
years, responds sympathetically to the
topography and existing mature trees of its
suburban site. The buildings are domestically scaled, but—as is typical of Bentley—
minimal in detail, blunt in profile, and
uniformly surfaced in light brown brick.
Stepped massing and the provision of screen
walls, enclosed garden courts, cedar pergolas, and external stairways—visible from
inside through large glazed openings—
endow Canavan Center with a delightful
intimacy, to which the extensive plantings
contribute substantially.

Rick Gardner

166 ★
UNITED SERVICES AUTOMOBILE
ASSOCIATION, 1975
9800 Fredricksburg Road
Benham-Blair & Affiliates

This vast insurance headquarters building,
1/3-mile in length, is located on a 300-acre
site. Containing three million square feet of
space and a 2,600-car underground garage,
USAA accommodates 6,000 employees.
The building is skewed in plan to conform
to the contour of the site. Inside, trays of
office space open onto an air-conditioned
three-story central court that runs the
length of the building. The architecture
results from construction and organization:
a composite system of precast concrete
panels cladding a light steel frame; recessed
ribbon windows; expressed stair towers; and
exposed air-handling units. A ranch house
and stable, existing on the property, were
adapted for company use. Neuhaus + Taylor
of Houston were interior architects; James
Keeter was landscape architect.

167 ★
UNIVERSITY BUSINESS PARK, 1985
12501 Network Boulevard
Rehler Vaughn Beaty & Koone

A deep-gridded fascia, accentuated with
contrasting colors, and staggered massing
give a distinctive identity to this 90,000-
square-foot office and service center. A 2½-
foot square grid was used as the dominant
visual element.

168 ★
THE UNIVERSITY OF TEXAS AT
SAN ANTONIO, 1976
6900 Loop 1604 West
Ford, Powell & Carson and
Bartlett Cocke & Associates

The oil-rich University of Texas System
commissioned a monumental institution
for its San Antonio campus, with a master
plan capable of accommodating 30,000 students at a remote hill-country site. Initially
5,000 students were instructed in five
academic colleges, occupying three
"superblocks" arranged around a central
plaza. The monolithic concrete buildings
are penetrated by interior courts and dramatic skylit hallways. Pedestrians are separated
from vehicular traffic by the elevated plaza,
which features a huge light-diffusing *som-
brilla* at its center and, along walkways,
wooden trellises hung from cables.

169 ★
MEDICAL CENTER TOWER, 1980
7950 Floyd Curl Street
The Marmon Mok Partnership

This 12-story office tower is faced with highly contrasted bands of white precast concrete and slot-ended ribbons of reflective glazing. Deep diagonal incisions are used to shape the building volumetrically, Houston-style, culminating in a glazed, wedge-roofed entrance lobby. Medical Center II (1986, Marmon Barclay Souter Foster Hays) is a companion piece.

170
ECUMENICAL CENTER, 1971 and 1978
4507 Medical Drive
Morris & McDonald

A small, economically built training center for pastoral care that serves the Southwest Texas Medical Center, this building consists of a series of shed-roofed volumes, picturesquely juxtaposed. Stepped-plan configurations, deeply shadowed bay openings, and the thrusting roof lines—culminating in a high-set clerestory—aim to give the center a sense of scale greater than its actual size.

171 ★
BALCONES HEIGHTS CITY HALL, 1971
111 Altgelt Street
Johnson-Dempsey & Associates

A diminutive municipal administration and police headquarters building set on a street of detached suburban houses, this city hall is in the O'Neil Ford style of Modernist regionalism. Counterposed shed roofs, the combination of variegated brown brick and cypress siding, and the unpretentious, almost domestic, scale of the building are all identifying characteristics.

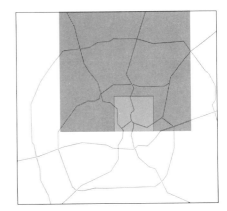

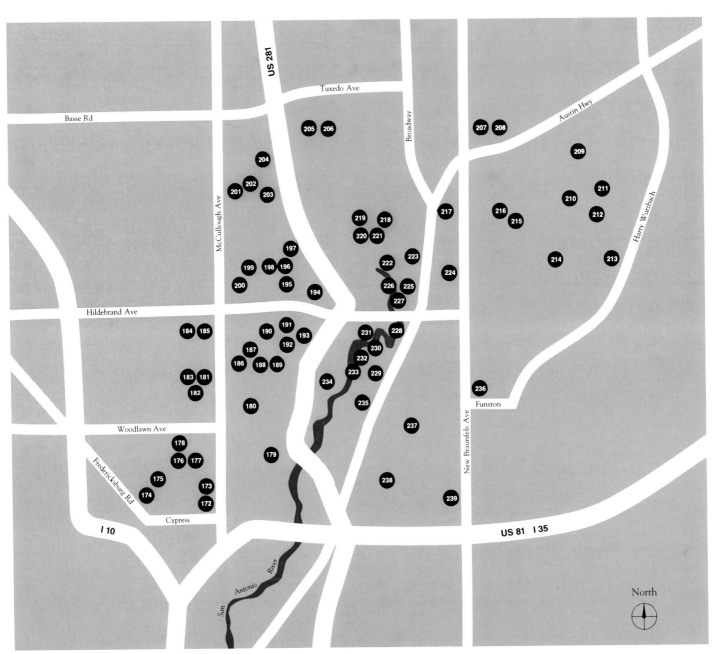

North

For connoisseurs of domestic architecture
between 1900 and 1940, north-central San
Antonio is a sheer delight. The area contains
the largest and most distinguished collection of
early- to mid-20th-century residential design in
all of Texas, spread throughout the neighborhoods of Monte Vista, Laurel Heights, Alamo
Heights, Olmos Park, and Terrell Hills. All
of the architects responsible for the revamping of
San Antonio's architectural character in the
1920s and 1930s designed houses here, and the
great majority of these works have survived
along with the broad streets and splendid landscaping that are so much a part of this special
environment. From bungalows to Spanish Colonial Revival-style haciendas on generous sites,
north-central San Antonio spans the full range
of residential architectural expression, and it
merits an extensive driving tour.

172
AURORA APARTMENTS, 1930
509 Howard Street
Richard van der Stratten and
    Herff & Jones

With Crockett Park as its front yard, the
Aurora takes full advantage of its site, lord-
ing over the entire neighborhood. The
flamboyant character of the exterior must
have seemed excessive at the start of the
Depression, but it results in a more dramatic
presence than that of its predecessor, the
Bushnell. While it now appears a little for-
lorn, the Aurora still carries all of the quasi-
Gothic terra-cotta balcony rails and cornice
enrichments that must have been designed
as a means of attracting prospective tenants.

173
HALFF HOUSE, 1908
601 Howard Street
Atlee B. Ayres
Restored 1985
Fisher, Heck Architects

One of the earliest extant houses by one of
the city's most important architects, the
Halff House illustrates the highly eclectic
character of Ayres's work before 1920. The
metal shingled roof, with its twin projections flanking the main entrance, seems
almost Japanese in character, but on a scale
that is entirely American. The arch framing
the front doors harkens back to the work of
H. H. Richardson and his numerous follow-
ers, especially in terms of the use of fine
materials like the polished grey granite
piers. The most original details are the columns of the first floor, with their quasi-Art
Nouveau foilate carving. Severely damaged
by a fire soon after restoration work had
begun, the house has been beautifully
returned to its original splendor.

174 ★
SAN ANTONIO TRANSIT SYSTEM
OFFICES, 1973
800 West Myrtle Avenue
Marmon & Mok Associates

A picturesque array of metal-surfaced shed
roofs and irregularly-spaced window openings in walls of tan brick identify this two-
story administration building, constructed
on a flat site facing San Pedro Park, with
the Modern regionalist look that O'Neil
Ford was instrumental in popularizing in
San Antonio. A pinwheel-plan configuration and diagonal alignments induce a sense
of visual movement. The large rectangular
windows and sloping roofs imbue the building with a surprisingly domestic character.

175 NR
SAN PEDRO SPRINGS PARK
1500 San Pedro Avenue

A lush site inhabited since prehistoric
times, land around the springs was declared
a public space by the Spanish in 1729. The
setting has served local activities for hun-
dreds of years as an Indian village, a Spanish
fort and mission, military camps and, since
1852, as a municipal park. Traditionally a
favorite gathering place for families, the
park is the former site of a museum, a zoo, a
bathhouse, and a tropical garden. An old
bandstand serves as a reminder of a more
glorious past.

176
TEMPLE BETH-EL, 1927
211 Belknap
Seutter & Simons

This striking structure and the Aurora are the most visible monuments of this largely low-scale residential neighborhood. The design of Temple Beth-El deftly combines square and spherical forms, unified by the consistent use of terra-cotta ornament and clay tiles. In this most Spanish of Texas cities, even a synagogue is designed with decidedly Iberian-Renaissance-style ornament, most notably the marvelous cornice composed of scallop shells. The contrast between the earth tones of the tiled dome and the whitewashed stucco of the exterior is no small part of this building's appeal.

177
KOEHLER HOUSE, 1900
310 West Ashby Street
Carl von Seutter

The extravagant Koehler House proves that not all of the wealthy German families of San Antonio lived on King William Street. Otto Koehler arrived in San Antonio from St. Louis in 1884 and later became one of the directors of the San Antonio Brewing Association—a very lucrative business indeed if his residence is any indication. The architect had worked for James Riely Gordon, but on this design he turned away from the polychromed Romanesque of his mentor toward a more free-spirited and individual style. The house benefits from its grand site, which occupies an entire city block.

178
ADAMS HOUSE, 1890
505 Belknap
McAdoo & Worley

This delightful compact extravaganza was
constructed as the residence of the
developer of the surrounding Laurel Heights
neighborhood. Fortunately, all of the components of the design have survived with
little change, including the ornamental
fence, the splendid carriage house, and the
remarkable railing on the front porch. The
metal griffins flanking the porch steps are
among the finest late-19th-century architectural details in San Antonio.

179
ST. SOPHIA GREEK ORTHODOX
CHURCH, 1926
2504 North St. Mary's Street
Emmett T. Jackson

San Antonio's Greek immigrants had worshipped with a visiting priest at St. Mark's
Episcopal Church, but the community grew
after World War I and raised enough money
to build its own church by 1926. Jackson's
Byzantine Revival design was successfully
detailed with inlaid tile, fine brickwork and
cast-stone pieces. A tile mosaic in the central arch over the entry depicts the double-
headed eagle of the ancient Byzantine
Empire. An interior apse screen was
imported from Greece. Icons on the barrel-
vaulted interior were painted by long-time
pastor Ergon J. Zografos; stained glass windows were installed in the 1960s.

180 ★
RUBLE CENTER OF TRINITY BAPTIST
CHURCH, 1983
401-405 East Magnolia Avenue
Chumney, Jones & Kell

The adaptive reuse of this former neighborhood school as an annex to Trinity Baptist
Church (1960, Bartlett Cocke) is a minor
work of virtuosity. Low-cost industrial
building components were assembled in a
lively, articulate manner, especially in the
design of a large multipurpose room inserted
in an L-shaped crook at the back of the
building. A pre-engineered metal shed, this
addition is faced with a shimmering screen
of glass block set in a brightly colored arma-
ture of exposed steel sections. On the street
elevation, only the panels of glass block in
the old loggia openings hint at the dramatic
transformations behind.

181
KAMPMANN HOUSE, 1922
131 East Kings Highway
Henry T. Phelps

This is a puzzle house, with one distinct portion—the main entrance arch—being from the residence of Herman Kampmann, built around 1890. Fortunately, the Kampmann family chose to save this fragment from the earlier house, preserving a fine piece of Richardsonian Romanesque stonework. Henry T. Phelps's integration of the arch into his design is highly successful as a dramatic contrast to the newer unadorned limestone wall surfaces. The handling of the projecting bay on the east elevation of the house is particularly effective.

182
McNEEL HOUSE, 1925
126 East Kings Highway
The Kelwood Company

Set far back from the street by a verdant lawn, the McNeel residence provides us with one local firm's interpretation of the Spanish Colonial Revival style. The rambling nature of such houses by the Ayres firm is not present here; the house is more blocklike, the only break coming with the large porte-cochere. The characteristic Spanish Colonial love of texture is provided by the barrel-tile roof and the Plateresque ornament set above the main entrance. While not in the same league as the firm's masterpieces, the Casino Club and Aztec Theater, this is nevertheless an impressive work.

183
HORNADAY HOUSE, 1929
101 East Kings Highway
Ralph Cameron

In the context of San Antonio architecture, Ralph Cameron is not well known for his residential work. Yet, he made the most of this particular opportunity. On the surface, this is a fairly typical piece of Colonial Revival work, except for the incredible front entrance. The almost-Baroque daring with which the architect recesses the door behind the monumental broken-pediment Palladian entry screen enhances the entire design. Against the power of the entrance, the paneled shutters with their jigsaw cutouts appear almost whimsical by comparison.

184
STOWERS HOUSE, 1925
131 West Lynwood Avenue
Adams & Adams

Yet another variant of the ever-popular Spanish Colonial Revival style, the Stowers House relies on changes in fenestration to emphasize the asymmetrical nature of the style. The inset entrance, with its extremely attenuated Solomonic columns, is the sole penetration into the mass of the house, while the polygonal bay forming its east end attempts to break out of the generally rectangular form. Given the extraordinary character of this firm's Thomas Jefferson High School, one would expect more imagination with respect to their residential works.

185
KOKERNOT HOUSE, 1928
115 East Lynnwood Avenue
Russell Brown Company

While not as grandiose as the Morgan House on Alameda Circle by the same firm, the Kokernot House is more accessible by virtue of its site placement. Once again the Spanish Colonial Revival asserts itself as the dominant style of the 1920s in the more affluent suburban neighborhoods. The Kokernot family built many other houses in this area.

186
HOGG HOUSE, 1924
202 Bushnell Avenue
Atlee B. & Robert M. Ayres

This house occupies a special place in the oeuvre of a noted San Antonio architectural firm. It is the first great work in the Spanish Colonial Revival style with which Atlee B. Ayres would be most strongly associated during the coming decade. The massing of the house is focused on the monumental cylindrical stair tower, which serves as the hinge on which the plan pivots. The austere character of the elevations is highlighted by some splendid details, most notably the massive front door, with its tiny window barred in wrought iron. The house was expanded by the firm in the 1950s when a series of rooms was added to the east end, but the character of the original design was maintained.

187
MANNEN HOUSE, 1926
323 Bushnell Avenue
Atlee B. & Robert M. Ayres

When designing houses in the Spanish Colonial Revival style, the Ayres firm made
consistent use of angled plans, resulting in
two masses meeting in an obtuse angle. The
Mannen residence is one of the smaller of
this breed, but it is characteristically well-
detailed. The arcaded verandah on the
ground floor and the wood balcony wrap-
ping around the second are the most regionally appropriate elements. The original
character of the facade openings to the right
of the doorway has been changed significantly by the installation of fixed sheets of
plate glass.

188 NR
THE BUSHNELL APARTMENTS, 1916
240 Bushnell Avenue
The Kelwood Company, Robert B. Kelly
Rehabilitated, 1982
Rehler, Vaughn, Beaty & Koone

The Kelwood Company, consisting of
architect Kelly and partner H.C. Wood,
built this seven-story apartment building as
an affluent dwelling in the fashionable hills
north of the city. The reinforced-concrete
structure is clad with stucco and cast-stone
details of Spanish Colonial Revival influence. The neighborhood now borders on
Trinity University and has maintained an
exclusive atmosphere. The apartments were
recently renovated with the intention to
sell as condominiums.

189 ★
UNIVERSITY PRESBYTERIAN
CHURCH, 1954
524 Shook
Milton A. Ryan

With characteristic ingenuity Ryan
designed this small church to make the most
of a low budget and readily available materials. The shape of the roof, the mullion
cross of the glazed central bay, and the organ
loft, displayed beneath the peak of the
steeply-pitched roof, identify the building
as a church; its pink-red brick surfaces relate
it visually to the adjacent buildings of Trinity University. Ryan also designed the
attached Education Building (1955). The
color of the painted elements is a recent,
unflattering alteration.

Trinity University

The Trinity campus consists of more than 45 buildings spread across a dramatic landscape that was once a limestone quarry. Adherence to an early master plan has assured that administrative and academic buildings occupy the high ground, and dormitories and athletic fields utilize the plain below. Buildings are oriented for optimum natural light and ventilation, and situated to blend with abundant native live oaks and mountain laurels. Innovative construction techniques have been utilized over the years to minimize costs. Some campus buildings were raised by pouring the upper floor slabs on the base and lifting them into place. The soaring brick bell tower serving as a campus campanile was built as a bearing-wall structure from the ground up. The university has developed a keen interest in energy conservation, adorning its buildings with solar collectors and experimenting with passive energy efficiency. The same pinkish exterior brick, coupled with details crafted by local artisans, have served as unifying elements for the campus' diverse collection of buildings.

190
SELIGMANN HOUSE, 1925
(Holt Center)
106 Oakmont
The Kelwood Company, Robert B. Kelly
Adaptive Reuse, 1982
DeLara-Almond

The Seligmann House, adapted in 1982 for use as the William Knox Holt Continuing Education Center, represents Kelly's approach to the Spanish Colonial Revival style on a grand scale. While Kelly seemed happy with more modest houses, such as the McNeel House on Kings Highway, he had difficulty in making the step up to really monumental residences. The massing of the Seligmann House has a kind of awkwardness that recalls the stage-set design that Kelly drew upon with such great success in a different context—the Aztec Theatre downtown.

191 ★
ELIZABETH COATES MADDUX
LIBRARY, 1979
Trinity University
Ford, Powell & Carson and
    Bartlett Cocke & Associates

This unusually programmed, four-story, 180,000-square-foot building is set in a hollow below surrounding campus buildings. To compensate for this anomaly, it is entered on its third-floor level, the lower two floors having been constructed to accommodate future expansion of the library's collection. The two upper levels of the reinforced concrete-framed building are finished in brick. Accentuating the serrated profile of the cruciform-planned building are glazed corner bays that harbor reading nooks.

Trinity University

Rick Gardner

Rick Gardner

192 ★
RUTH TAYLOR THEATER, 1966
Trinity University
O'Neil Ford & Associates and
    Bartlett Cocke & Associates

In conjunction with the Chapman Graduate
Center (1965) just to the west, the Ruth
Taylor Theater marked Ford's turn toward a
Modern regionalist vernacular, of which
the Ruth Taylor's standing-seam metal-
covered shed-roofed masses, segmental
arches, slit windows, and fanciful brick
detail all were attributes. Working with
Trinity's famed theatrical director, Paul
Baker, Ford and his associate Arthur J.
Rogers designed the building to house three
distinct theater spaces. Baker insisted upon
flexible, readily adaptable performance and
work spaces. But he was emphatic that the
architects produce a "masterpiece of space,"
not just a bland, neutral container. One
level below the campus street is a handsome
patio garden, shared with Richardson Hall,
to the east.

193 ★
LAURIE AUDITORIUM, 1971
Trinity University
Ford, Powell & Carson and
    Bartlett Cocke & Associates

Laurie Auditorium consists of a partially-
exposed drum-like substructure of reinforced concrete containing a 300-car garage; a fan-shaped, copper-clad superstruc-
ture containing a 3,000-seat auditorium;
and the Sid W. Richardson Communica-
tions Center, a brick-faced, shed-roofed
classroom building oriented toward the
courtyard of the Ruth Taylor Center. The
massive semicircular structure was set on a
steeply sloping downhill site to minimize
the impact of its bulk on the campus, while

giving it a public aspect from East Hilde-
brand Avenue to the north. The garage, its
interstitial bays filled with vertical cedar
slats, provides a terrace for the auditorium
above.

194
FRANK MURCHISON HOUSE, 1939
9 Ironwood Road
O'Neil Ford & Arch B. Swank, Jr.

O'Neil Ford's first building commission in San Antonio was for this horizontally extended one- and two-story house of stone and cedar. The house is pulled out, one room deep, across its sloping site. Ford and Swank turned its back to the street while opening the garden elevation to the downhill slope and the prevailing breeze. The shallowly pitched copper roof; the blind, gabled end walls with exposed, stone chimney stacks; and the cantilevered, south-facing balcony recall the mid-19th-century building traditions of San Antonio and central Texas. The horizontality and openness of the house, however, identify it as Modern in the spirit of the American Regionalist movement of the 1930s.

195
ROBERTSON HOUSE, 1930
303 Devine Road
William McKnight Bowman

Along with the Webb and Newton Houses around the corner on East Olmos Drive, the Robertson House forms what is likely the finest trio of late 1920s residences in San Antonio. Bowman's design, which was prominently featured in the April 1930 issue of *The Architectural Forum*, takes its inspiration from the great villas of the Veneto, although at a much smaller scale. In the true tradition of the Italian villa, the second floor contains the greatest room, a vast drawing room that bisects the second floor and is apparent on the exterior in the form of the arcaded loggia overlooking the sweeping front lawn. The only element needed to complete the mood is a body of water replacing Devine Road.

196
JONES HOUSE, 1927
810 East Olmos Drive
Atlee B. & Robert M. Ayres

The formal symmetry of the Jones house makes for an interesting comparison to the adjacent Newton house, both coming from the same year. Actually, it is an enlarged version of a house designed by Ayres & Ayres five years earlier, but on a much larger site than its prototype. The concentration of ornament around the entrance portico is judiciously balanced by the rather austere character of the rest of the exterior walls.

197
SLICK HOUSE, 1959
400 Devine Road
O'Neil Ford & Associates

All but invisible from the street, this
extremely large one-story house, contained
beneath a concrete lift-slab roof, was
designed by Ford for one of his most important patrons, Thomas B. Slick, Jr. The walls
are laid up in dry-stacked Vallecillo stone;
the entry is shielded by a solar screen of clay
tile; and parked cars in front of the house
are sheltered beneath a marvelous,
sculptural "carport" of tubular steel. The
expansive grounds, which look out across
the Olmos Basin to Alamo Heights, were
designed by the landscape architect Arthur
S. Berger.

198
NEWTON HOUSE, 1927
800 East Olmos Drive
Atlee B. & Robert M. Ayres

With its beautifully landscaped site, the
Newton House is one of the best efforts of
the Ayres firm. While this is a large house,
there is an informality apparent in the seemingly random placement of the fenestration
on the outside walls. The entrance tower
hints at the design of the Atkinson residence, which was to follow on the heels of
the Newton commission. The sculptural
molding that frames the front door is
unusual in the firm's work and adds an element of three-dimensionality to the otherwise flat surfaces of the walls.

199
WILLIAMSON HOUSE, 1968
303 Park Hill Drive
Flowers & Maxwell

Exterior wall faces and turns reveal the simple interior plan of this residence, nestled into a mature landscape of tall oaks and lush ground cover. Individual rooms radiate like a series of shed-roofed pavilions around a 2-story core. Vertical accents rival the trees through tall chimneys of Mexican brick, board-and-batten siding of stained cedar, slender window units, and banks of French doors. Yet the horizontal earth is confirmed by the gently sloping roofs covered with flat Saltillo tiles. The combined effect reveals a contemporary interpretation of the Arts and Crafts Movement from the early 1900s.

200
TURNER HOUSE, 1928
214 Park Hill Drive
Robert H. H. Hugman

The Turner House is one of the gems of Olmos Park and of San Antonio at large. While well known for the design of the Paseo del Rio, Hugman was clearly capable of more than stage-set architecture. This is one of the best Spanish Colonial Revival houses in the city, combining the monumental simplicity of the 18th-century originals and the inventiveness of the revival. The highlight of the house is the small room topped by a dome on scroll brackets, which appears to have been copied from the great mission church of San Xavier del Bac near Tucson, a structure Hugman surely knew and admired.

201
MORGAN HOUSE, 1929
300 Alameda Circle
Russell Brown Company

What makes the Morgan House such a testimonial to the abilities of the architects who designed it is how well it conceals its enormous size from the passerby. The house, a low-key Mediterranean villa, contains more than 20,000 square feet of living area. The house is set back from the traffic circle it faces, and the growth of the trees has further screened it from the eyes of the curious.

203
NEGLEY HOUSE, 1929
300 Paseo Encinal
George Louis Walling

202
CLEMENTS HOUSE, 1947
505 East Mandalay Drive
Birdsall P. Briscoe

Briscoe, one of Houston's most assured eclectic architects, excelled at Southern regionalized versions of the neo-Adam and Regency genres. This house, designed in 1941 but not begun until 1946, exemplifies his grand manner, with its noble, south-facing portico looking out across a terraced garden toward East Wildwood Drive, and its scarcely less honorific north-facing motor-court elevation. Briscoe even pressed the garage into this double-fronted composition so that it serves as an architectural terminus for cross axes that traverse the east garden. This ranks as one of Olmos Park Estates' outstanding Georgian-style houses.

The Negley House benefits from one of the loveliest sites in Olmos Park. In its heavily wooded setting, the house seems a natural part of the landscape. Curiously, the architect was from Austin, an unusual circumstance considering the prominence of the Negley family in San Antonio. The stone for the walls came from the old Washer Store downtown, which accounts for the fact that the house appears to be much older than its construction date.

204
SEELIGSON HOUSE, 1939
835 Contour Drive
John F. Staub

Houston's foremost eclectic architect, John
F. Staub, designed this monumental stone
country house as a regionalized, suburbanized French chateau. Its symmetrical
main block is flanked by low, shed-roofed
appendages that extend outward to tie the
house to its site. Oriented to take advantage
of the prevailing breeze and downhill views,
the house reveals both its entrance and garden elevations to passers-by.

205
ST. LUKE'S EPISCOPAL CHURCH,
1955
11 St. Luke's Lane
Henry Steinbomer

On the ridge of Alamo Heights overlooking
the Olmos Basin, Steinbomer sited a formidable complex of buildings for this Angli-
can parish, designed in a mannered "contemporary" version of neo-Gothic. The
lofty interior of the church, lit through
extensive panels of stained glass executed

by Cecil Casebier, is carried on laminated
wood members. Steinbomer's extremely
attenuated bell tower and spire are highly
visible, especially from the McAllister
Freeway.

206
LANG HOUSE, 1953
700 Alta Avenue
Harwell Hamilton Harris

After Harris came to Texas in 1951 to become director of the School of Architecture at The University of Texas, he designed a number of houses across the state. This was one of several inspired by Frank Lloyd Wright's Usonian houses of the 1930s and '40s. Vertically accentuated pink-brick panels bracket horizontal expanses of lapped wood siding that serve as fascias above banked windows. Reticent on its public side, the house opens out to its south-facing rear garden and the downhill slope.

207
MARION KOOGLER MCNAY
MUSEUM, 1928
6000 North New Braunfels Avenue
Atlee B. & Robert M. Ayres
Additions, 1970, 1973, 1975, 1982
Ford, Powell & Carson

One of the cultural centers of San Antonio, the McNay represents the work of two of the city's most noted architectural firms. The residence commissioned by the Atkinsons marks the apogee of the series of Spanish Colonial Revival style houses by the Ayres firm that had begun in 1923 with the Thomas Hogg House on Bushnell Avenue. The design of the house, which was significantly influenced by the taste of Marion Atkinson, later Marion Koogler McNay, centered around the great enclosed patio with walled pool and planting beds. On her death in 1950, the estate was converted into a museum displaying her personal art collection. The expansion of the museum facilities that began in 1970 has retained much of the feel of the Atkinson residence, especially in the patio. Fortunately, the house came with ample grounds that could readily accommodate such an expansion, grounds that included the large fountain facing the main entrance tower of the original house. The quality of the detailing of the house is worthy of close scrutiny, especially the wrought-iron work and the extensive use of Spanish-decorated tiles.

209
BENTLEY HOUSE, 1982
511 Morningside Drive
Ken Bentley and Associates

The second dwelling Bentley built for himself, this tan brick house consists of a series
of box-like masses configured around protected outdoor spaces. Thin stone belt
courses accentuate the horizontality of the
facade screen, which is pierced by two bays
of cast-stone louvers to maintain privacy
without blocking the prevailing breeze.

208
SAN ANTONIO ART INSTITUTE, 1979
6000 North New Braunfels Avenue
Flowers & Maxwell

Stepped and curved screen walls of light
brown brick, capped by heavy molded brick
copings, give the Art Institute building an
ambiguous, rather mysterious external
aspect, while affording north-facing studios
generous, protected garden courts. The
venturi-shaped entrance bay occasions a
tour-de-force in fictile masonry work: stout
brick columns with elaborate bases and capitals, corbelled brick piers, and radiating
brick paving, all dominated by the heavy,
notched wooden *portales* that shade the
north and south entrance courts.

210
OAK COURT—
H. LUTCHER BROWN ESTATE, 1936
636 Ivy Lane
Atlee B. & Robert M. Ayres

Without question the greatest house in San Antonio by this important firm, Oak Court represents the climax of a decade of outstanding residential design that began with the Thomas Hogg House in 1924. The form and scale of the house result from a close partnership between Robert M. Ayres and H. Lutcher Brown, whose fortune was derived from forests and paper mills in Louisiana and who greatly admired that state's plantation houses. While not a replica of any colonial or ante-bellum structure, the house borrows details from such distinguished sources as the Mathias Hammond House in Annapolis, whose doorframe inspired the enlarged version dominating the front elevation of the Brown house. The original 24-acre site has been reduced by ten acres, but all of the original outbuildings and landscaping have been retained.

211 ★
SCHERR HOUSE, 1953
105 Newberry Terrace
Milton A. Ryan

Together with its next-door neighbor at 111, this house exemplifies Ryan's deft, constructivist approach to Modern architecture. Economy and exposition of structure, maximum lightness and transparency, unassertive massing, and responsiveness to sloping sites characterize these adjoining houses. Both are splendidly maintained and have been spared the crude alterations with which subsequent owners have so frequently spoiled Ryan's delightful, delicate houses.

212
JOHN MURCHISON HOUSE, 1941
939 Garraty Road
O'Neil Ford

Designed for the brother of Ford's first San Antonio client, Frank Murchison, this two-story house of variegated pink brick and cedar is even larger (20 rooms, 12,000 square feet) and more expansive. Set atop the crest of a low, wooded hill, it is one room deep, elongated horizontally in thin wings. Since the prevailing breeze and favored views were toward the public street rather than away from it, the main entrance is from a motor court at the rear of the house and the downhill slope is preserved as a sweeping garden. Since steel was in scarce supply when the house was built, Murchison used oil-sucker rods from oil rigs for the 45-foot steel piers beneath the foundation.

214
CHITTIM HOUSE, 1922
501 Elizabeth Road
Atlee B. & Robert M. Ayres

213 ★
DUNWOODY HOUSE, 1951
735 Elizabeth Road
Milton A. Ryan

Milton Ryan described this ethereal house as his "pipe dream." Horizontal steel angles welded to a network of steel pipe columns and struts anchor the floating roof and floor planes. Sandwiched in between, the walls alternate betweeen panels of redwood plywood and fixed and operable glazing units. Taking advantage of the sloping site, Ryan placed a carport beneath the house; the front door is approached from ground level by a "gangplank" ramp and a boomerang-shaped terrazo terrace. This is one of six houses that Ryan designed and built speculatively in the 600 and 700 blocks of Elizabeth Road between 1948 and 1951. All radiate the enthusiasm and ingenuity he brought to the practice of Modern architecture.

One of the earlier houses in Terrell Hills, the Chittim residence benefits from its large and beautifully landscaped site—an irresistibly idyllic setting. An unusual one-story design from the Ayres's firm, the Chittim House makes extensive use of shelter-giving verandahs, which are framed by a series of columns with Mudejar-style capitals.

215
STEVES HOUSE, 1965
501 Grandview Place
O'Neil Ford & Associates

This is a splendid, romantic house, a latter-day evocation of the Spanish Governor's Palace translated to a small suburban estate. In plan the 14,000-square-foot house is Modern, consisting of pavilion units projected from a lateral, 100-foot-long gallery and interspersed with patio gardens. Its traditional aspect derives from architectural artifacts—such as the massive entrance portal and doors and the stone coping along the tops of the walls—which the owners acquired in Mexico and which Chris Carson judiciously incorporated into the design of the house. Mexican masons were imported to lay up the internal brick vaulting. Like the landscaped courtyards, this interior richness is concealed behind austere exterior walls. Stewart E. King & Associates were landscape architects.

216
WINTER HOUSE, 1981
400 Wiltshire
Ford, Powell & Carson

Located just around the corner from the firm's better-known residence for Marshall Steves, the Winter House is a more informal and congenial work. The large size of the site permits a rambling plan comprised of one-story units framing an entrance courtyard. The vistas out of the house are all oriented away from the street, with the exception of the rooftop terrace, clearly identified by the trellis. For this residence, Chris Carson turned to the domestic architecture of Greece for his inspiration, proving that there is room for more than just one type of regional expression in San Antonio.

217
MAGNOLIA OIL COMPANY, 1930
5424 Broadway
Architect unknown

Occupying a key site on one of the city's most important thoroughfares, this structure harks back to a time when the servicing of an automobile was the responsibility of a large staff. The famous flying horse emblem and the romantic tiled roof have become neighborhood landmarks through the years. While tradition claims this to be the work of the Ayres firm, there is no positive documentation. The design could well have originated within the corporate structure of the oil company.

218 ★
LIGHT HOUSE, 1962
300 Argyle Avenue
Brooks Martin & Associates

At first glance, this unobtrusive, yet dramatic, house appears to consist only of a trans-
parent pavilion floating in a suburban garden. Closer examination reveals a low,
backup wing, *L*-shaped in plan, to which
the pavilion is discretely attached. Tan-col-
ored brick, cedar siding and posts, and the
crisp rectilinearity of the overhanging roof
decks are in the San Antonio tradition of
Modernist regionalism.

219
THE ARGYLE, 1854
734 Patterson Avenue
Remodeled, 1884

Originally the center of a large horse ranch,
the Argyle arrived at its present form in the
mid-1880s. The house was at that time
acquired by two Scotsmen, who operated
the enlarged and embellished structure as a
hotel that was named for their home county
in Scotland. Predating all of its Alamo
Heights neighbors by at least 40 years, the
Argyle is now used as a private social club
benefitting the Southwest Foundation for
Research and Education.

220
MAVERICK-ZACHRY HOUSE, 1929
401 Torcido Drive
George Washington Smith

This is the only work in Texas by the noted
architect who was responsible for creating
the Santa Barbara style using the forms of
Spanish Colonial architecture. Well-
screened from the road by the trees that
have grown up alongside it, the house is
arranged around a large central courtyard,
with access from the outside provided by
the simple doorframe set in the otherwise
planar exterior wall. Smith, who was to die
before the completion of the house, tended
to rely on less complicated massing than did
many who practiced in this style, and his
skills are evident in this, one of San
Antonio's best 20th-century houses.

221
SCHOENBAUM HOUSE, 1985
400 Torcido Drive
Isaac Maxwell

Schoenbaum means beautiful tree in German, and the clients here chose to build a house befitting their name. The structure is carefully nestled among native vegetation, with the entry stair and retaining walls creating additional space for plantings. The house folds over its site with double-wythe walls of handmade Mexican brick, highlighted by standing-seam metal roofing and terrace paving of Arkansas ledgestone. The architect designed and made all light fixtures, doors, panels, and other details, giving the house what he calls "contemporary regional" detailing.

222
CONDOMINIUMS AT
200 PATTERSON, 1985
200 Patterson Avenue
Callaway, Hylton & Garison

The only mid-rise building in Alamo Heights, this all-white, 11-story condominium apartment building was secluded in a wooded estate setting to quell considerable opposition to its construction in a neighborhood formerly restricted to single-family houses. Partially screened from view by mature trees along Patterson Avenue, the building has staggered massing and insistent scalloped parapets that give it a marked presence from McAllister Freeway.

223
BUS STOP, circa 1929
Broadway at Patterson
Dionicio Rodriguez, craftsman

This organic concoction has unflinchingly served transit riders for more than half a century. When maestro Rodriguez completed his steel-frame, tinted-concrete work here—donated to the city by San Antonio Portland Cement Co. (now Alamo Cement)—the shelter served trolleys. Since then the quiet neighborhood that once marked the division between Incarnate Word College and the residences of Alamo Heights has become a bustling shopping center. The tracks were removed about 1931, the street name has been changed from River Street to Broadway, and the road has been widened to six lanes plied by impatient autos and fuming buses.

224 ★
LA QUINTA APARTMENTS, 1964
185 Terrell Road
Chris Carson

La Quinta is a 24-unit complex of row
houses on two contiguous corner lots, built
above depressed parking and focused
inwardly on austere, enclosed communal
spaces. Wall planes on sand-surfaced brick
punctuated by segmentally-arched door and
window openings ally these houses with the
Modern regionalist vernacular promoted by
Carson's associate, O'Neil Ford. James Keeter was responsible for the landscape design.

225
INCARNATE WORD COLLEGE
CHAPEL AND CONVENT, 1900
4301 Broadway
F.B. Gaenslen
Chapel added 1907

In a city dominated by the stuccoed forms of
the Spanish Colonial period and its 20th-
century revival, the bright orange brick of
these ecclesiastical landmarks is a welcome
surprise. There is something rather Gallic
about this pair, especially the chapel, which
resembles, albeit on a small scale, some of
the vast unbuilt projects to come out of the
Ecole des Beaux-Arts in Paris. Of special
interest are the trumpeting angels on the
corners of the bell tower, clearly cribbed
from similar figures executed by Frederic
Auguste Bartholdi on the tower of H.H.
Richardson's Brattle Square Church in Boston of the early 1870s. These are the earliest
structures erected on the campus of Incarnate Word College, whose land was once
part of Col. G. W. Brackenridge's estate.

226 NR
FERNRIDGE, circa 1852, 1886
(Brackenridge Villa)
Jules Poinsard
Renovated, 1985
Robert Callaway

Sited on a wooded hill above the San
Antonio River's headwaters, the east wing
of this rambling structure was built after
1852 by city mayor James R. Sweet. The
large, raised one-story cottage features
Greek Revival symmetry and detailing.
Local entrepreneur George Washington
Brackenridge bought the property in 1869,
named the 280-acre estate "Alamo
Heights," and built the large Queen-Anne
style west wing in 1886. Both wings apparently received a stucco finish sometime
later. The Sisters of Charity of the Incarnate
Word bought the entire estate in 1897 and
built Incarnate Word College near the residence. Renovation was interrupted in 1983
by a fire and heavy damage.

227
BETTY HUTH MADDUX THEATER,
1980
Incarnate Word College
4301 Broadway
Ford, Powell & Carson

The first new structure erected on the Incarnate Word campus in 20 years, the Maddux
Theater breaks from the campus tradition of
brick-faced buildings with its bush-ham-
mered concrete walls that recall the cast-
stone lintels and sills used throughout the
campus. Sited at the rear of a public plaza,
and flanked by earlier structures, the building contains a 270-seat proscenium theater
that is linked by a two-story lobby to an
experimental theater seating 150. The
project also called for the renovation of an
existing early 20th-century classroom building for use as a dance rehearsal hall and dress-
ing room.

228 ★
UNITED SERVICES AUTOMOBILE
ASSOCIATION, 1955
(Southwestern Bell Telephone Building)
4119 Broadway
Phelps & Dewees & Simmons and
    Atlee B. & Robert M. Ayres

The USAA's second purpose-built headquarters, like its eventual successor (#166),
is massive in size, relatively low in height
(seven and eight stories), and suburban in
location. It is also a spectacular 1950s period
piece. Composition, fenestration, and
materials change with orientation; color
contrasts (white Georgian marble and tur-
quoise porcelain enamel spandrel panels)
are intense.

Brackenridge Park

Parts of the 5800-acre Brackenridge Park comprise an original Spanish land grant to the city. Another tract had been sold in 1863 by the city to the Confederate government for a tannery, then was confiscated by the Union Army in 1865, and bought back by the city in 1868. But the San Antonio Waterworks Company—wholly owned by Colonel George Washington Brackenridge—gave a huge tract along the San Antonio River to the city in 1899, and the park was thereafter named for the benefactor. Numerous other land acquisitions and improvements have been added by the city in subsequent years. The zoo was established in 1919, developing into a complex of open-air pens, pathways, waterways, and support facilities. Thomas Pressly's 1967 bird house resembles both a medieval chapter house and a railroad roundhouse, with "chapels" or "stalls" radiating from a central clerestory hub and housing exotic fowl in "native" environments. The 1979 Children's Zoo is distributed through several pavilions with indoor and outdoor "native" vignettes, and includes a waterway with boat rides.

229
PIONEER HALL, 1937
(Texas Ranger Museum)
3805 Broadway
Atlee B. & Robert M. Ayres and
    Phelps & Dewees

The museum is one of several buildings constructed locally with the assistance of the State of Texas to commemorate the centennial of Texas independence. Its boldly scaled, full-bodied, yet simple Renaissance classical detail owes much to the example of Paul Philippe Cret, whose post office on Alamo Plaza and whose campus buildings at The University of Texas in Austin were newly completed. In front of the museum is a bronze cast of the maquette of Gutzon Borglum's *Trail Drivers Memorial*; the full-scale piece was never executed. Next door, at 3801 Broadway, is the Witte Museum. The Mediterranean original (1926 and 1930, Atlee B. & Robert M. Ayres) is concealed by the blandly Modernistic front gallery addition.

230
IRON BRIDGE, 1890
San Antonio River in Brackenridge Park
Berlin Iron Bridge Company,
    East Berlin, Connecticut

This iron truss bridge was one of four assembled in 1890-91 to span the San Antonio River downtown. This specimen originally served St. Mary's Street but was later replaced by a sturdier span. It was refurbished in the park by National Youth Administration labor in 1937-38. The other three bridges were recently restored by the city and still serve downtown traffic at Presa, Crockett, and Convent Streets.

Brackenridge Park

231
BATH HOUSES, 1917
Brackenridge Park

A major man-made feature in the early years of Brackenridge Park was a swim beach on this bend of the San Antonio River. The Lambert Bathing Beach— named for a park commissioner of the period—is gone now, but the adjacent bathhouse remains. Its 40 stalls plus concession shelter were constructed of cast concrete, clad with a riverstone veneer. Scolloped window openings give the simple structure an air of sophistication. The roof over the concession stall is covered with clay tile, but the framing over the changing rooms was evidently secured only with wire mesh for thorough ventilation.

232
PEDESTRIAN BRIDGE, circa 1929
San Antonio River in Brackenridge Park
Dionicio Rodriguez, craftsman

This *faux bois* masterpiece, simulating an arbor of woven wooden limbs, is one of several pieces of molded concrete work by Rodriguez in San Antonio. The Mexican artisan was evidently brought to the city to work on Dr. Aureliana Urrutia's house, a fantastic showplace of folk art, unfortunately since razed. The pedestrian bridge and other similar works by Rodriguez in Brackenridge Park are thought to have been donated to the city by the San Antonio Portland Cement Company (now Alamo Cement), which once operated a quarry near the park.

233
JOSKE PAVILION, 1927
Brackenridge Park
Emmett T. Jackson

A spirit of whimsical exaggeration animates this stone-built park shelter and recreation building. The thick, battered walls, stout-beamed ceilings, and buttressed, polygonal chimney stack all contribute to an atmosphere of light-hearted, if tectonically dense, fantasy—as does the operatic stair at the north end of the pavilion, its landing spanning an arched recess that opens outward between chunky masonry colonettes.

234 NR
SUNKEN GARDENS
Brackenridge Park

Claimed to be the first Portland cement works in the Southwest, this old quarry supplied one of the largest cement producers in the world during the 1880s and 1890s. The site was converted by the city to the "Japanese Sunken Gardens" in 1917 with prison labor. After Pearl Harbor in 1941, the name was changed to "Chinese Sunken Gardens," and then later to "Oriental Sunken Gardens." A large brick smokestack and several lime kilns left from the cement works are preserved within the park.

235 ★
INTERCONTINENTAL MOTORS, 1960
(Lone Star Volkswagen)
3303 Broadway
O'Neil Ford & Associates

This exceptional auto showroom and maintenance building was designed to preserve 75 mature trees on its three-acre site and to assuage local indignation over demolition of Quinta Urrutia (1918), an unusual Mexican-style mansion that previously had occupied the property. The glazed, cruciform sales pavilion, elevated on a coved, back-lit base, was advanced forward of the maintenance block to fit in among the trees. In the interest of public acceptance for the building, Ford and his associate Howard Wong carefully detailed the exposed concrete structural components and the enclosing membrane of brick and glass to achieve a level of architectural refinement unusual among buildings of this type. The weaver and ceramicist Martha Mood was responsible for ornamental lighting fixtures and Lynn Ford executed the beaten-copper planting troughs.

236
SAN ANTONIO BOTANICAL CENTER, 1980
555 Funston Place
James E. Keeter and George G. Cook, Landscape Architects

Situated on a low hill in Ludwig Mahncke Park, the San Antonio Botanical Center encompasses 33 acres of thematically landscaped gardens, notably the Texas native area that features three different Texas regional ecologies: a Hill Country/ Edwards Plateau section at the center of the park, a Southwest Texas section on the east side, and an East Texas section on the north perimeter. In addition to plantings and landscape forms characteristic of these areas, representative historic building types were either moved intact or reconstructed in each sector.

237 ★
MULBERRY TERRACE APARTMENTS,
1960
1305 and 1315 East Mulberry Avenue
Allison B. Peery

Peery developed these two sets of 14-unit
garden apartments on a sloping site, floating
the rear blocks over parking stalls at the
downhill end of the property. Panelized wall
surfaces feature extensive glazing, and the
units are apportioned generous shares of
outdoor space enclosed with horizontal
wood-slat privacy screens. Exposed outdoor
stairs, cantilevered from brick planes, and a
network of pedestrian bridges animate the
common spaces. Stewart E. King and James
Keeter were landscape architects.

238 NR
PERSHING HOUSE, 1881
Fort Sam Houston, Staff Post Road
Alfred Giles

As Fort Sam Houston was developed into a
major military post in the 1880s, a series of
posh residences was built along Staff Post
Road to house high-ranking Army officers
and their families. All were served by stables
and servants' quarters at the rear. This
house is larger than the others, designed to
accommodate the commanding general of
all military installations in the region. The
walls are of limestone, trimmed with milled
wood and accented with a mansard-roofed
cupola. The frame gallery was a typical
regional necessity, later enclosed with
insect screens. General John Joseph Pershing once occupied the house, and his name
is commonly associated with it.

239 NR
THE QUADRANGLE, 1879
4 Park Hill Drive

The U.S. Army had supplied its forts on the
Texas frontier from San Antonio since
1847, first occupying the old Alamo buildings near the city center. By 1877 the Quartermaster Depot was moved to this facility
of limestone warehouses and shops enclosing a nine-acre plaza. The central tower of
limestone, serving as a water- and watch-
tower, was fitted with a clock in 1882.
Headquarters for the Fifth Army, Fort Sam
Houston is now a 35,000-acre complex surrounding these original buildings.

Nine San Antonio Architects

The architecture of the city is a process of evolution involving the overlapping ideas and influences of those architects who practice here. Following are brief profiles of nine architects whose careers, now ended, have been influential in shaping the architecture of San Antonio.

Photo credits: Francois Giraud and Robert M. Ayres courtesy of the Institute of Texan Cultures, San Antonio; James Wahrenberger, courtesy of the Daughters of the Republic of Texas Library at the Alamo; Atlee B. Ayres and Ralph Cameron courtesy of The Architectural Drawings Collection, the Architecture and Planning Library, University of Texas at Austin; George Willis courtesy of the San Antonio Light.

FRANCOIS PIERRE GIRAUD, 1818-1877

Giraud was a cosmopolitan gentleman who was enveloped by and no doubt contributed to San Antonio's international flair. He was born in Charleston, South Carolina, to French parents who sent him to Mt. St. Mary's College prep school in Maryland from 1830 to 1834. He later returned there to teach chemistry from 1842 to 1847.

He was trained as a metallurgy engineer at the *Ecole Centrale des Arts et Manufactures* in Paris, graduating in 1842. Giraud came to Texas in 1847, and by 1848 was the first city surveyor of San Antonio. While he worked on the first buildings at the Ursuline Academy, he surveyed the grounds of the five old Spanish missions, and helped the Catholic Church establish its claim to their ownership. In 1852 he persuaded the city to preserve San Pedro Springs as a city park.

During the Civil War, Giraud served as a Confederate captain of engineers, assigned as chief engineer of defenses at Galveston in 1865. He returned to work on Ursuline Academy in 1866, and began construction of the new San Fernando Cathedral in 1868.

As soon as Reconstruction ended in Texas, Giraud was able to hold public office and served as mayor of San Antonio from 1872 to retirement in 1875.

ALFRED GILES, 1853-1920

Born the seventh son of a wealthy Englishman, Alfred Giles apprenticed with a London firm and attended night courses at the University of London. He came to San Antonio in 1873, seeking a warmer climate for his rheumatic heart, and worked for master builder John H. Kampmann, who taught him the characteristics of local building materials.

By 1875 Giles had his own office, booming with San Antonio after the arrival of the railroad from Houston. He married Annie Laurie James in 1881 and had eight children; two sons later practiced architecture in his office. After his mother's death in 1885 in London, Giles retired briefly to England with his family. He soon sold his holdings there and returned to Texas in 1886.

That year Giles and his wife's family acquired several thousand acres of hill country west of San Antonio near Comfort. Giles was evidently content to develop the livestock ranch and pursue choice architectural commissions by lengthy commute, rather than regain what had been the foremost practice in San Antonio.

When railroads opened Mexico to the 20th century, Giles learned Spanish and opened a branch office in Monterrey. He produced numerous public buildings throughout Mexico before the 1914 revolution.

Giles died at his ranch while still actively heading the Alfred Giles Company in San Antonio.

JAMES WAHRENBERGER, 1855-1929

JAMES RIELY GORDON, 1864-1937

ATLEE B. AYRES, 1874-1969
ROBERT M. AYRES, 1898-1977

A native Texan born in Austin to parents of German descent, Wahrenberger was an early beneficiary of a European education. He was first sent at age 14 to Philadelphia to study at West Pennsylvania Academy, then in 1872 he journeyed to Zurich, Switzerland, to study mathematics. At Karlsruhe, Germany, he concentrated for three years on architecture at the Polytechnic Institute. After an extended tour of Europe, Wahrenberger returned to Austin.

Wahrenberger's proposal in 1881 for the new state capitol was judged second place. In 1882 he opened a practice in San Antonio with Albert Felix Beckman (1855-1900), who had also been educated in Germany. They acted as local architects for the St. Louis firm of E. Jugenfeld and Co. for the erection of the Lone Star Brewery after 1895.

A subsequent second-place award, for the Bexar County Courthouse in 1891, perhaps kept Wahrenberger from entering the mainstream of statewide practice. He maintained his Austin contacts, designing a Victorian fantasy home there in 1893 for George Washington Littlefield—arch rival of San Antonio's own G.W. Brackenridge.

Wahrenberger received several noteworthy commissions from Catholic groups at the turn of the century. He attained an elder statesman role in the San Antonio architecture community before his death at age 74.

Born in Virginia, Gordon moved to San Antonio with his railroad engineer father and family in the early 1870s. At age 16 he worked in a railroad engineering office, and then apprenticed to architect Wesley Clark Dodson in 1882. The next year he moved to Washington, D.C., to work for the Architect of the Treasury.

Gordon returned to San Antonio in 1887, initially supervising the construction of a massive new Romanesque Revival Post Office and Federal Building on Alamo Plaza. The Texas courthouse law of 1881—allowing counties to sell bonds for new courthouses—had created a healthy but competitive climate for architects in the state, and Gordon joined the bandwagon by 1890.

Italianate and Second Empire temples had been early favorites among county commissioners, but Gordon introduced massive Romanesque models. His standard design replaced the dainty pressed-metal cupola with a bearing-wall masonry tower, signaling drastic changes in the spatial plan beneath. Whereas the older wooden-frame cupola was mounted awkwardly on the ceiling of a central courtroom, Gordon's plan spun around the tower's hollow core, which acted as a circulation chimney and stair well.

Gordon designed the award-winning Texas Pavilion at the 1893 Chicago World's Fair, and the 1900 Arizona Territorial Capitol at Phoenix. He moved his practice to New York in 1904.

Atlee B. Ayres arrived in San Antonio with his parents in 1880, and was to have a lasting impact upon the architecture of the city for the first half of the 20th century. After attending courses at the Art Students League and the Metropolitan School of Art in New York City, Ayres returned to San Antonio and entered into a partnership with C. A. Coughlin that lasted until Coughlin's death in 1905. In the next 15 years, the elder Ayres designed numerous residences, including those for Alex Halff and the now-demolished villa for Col. George W. Brackenridge. Large-scale commissions from this period include First Presbyterian Church and the Heimann Building. The 1920s brought two major changes: the establishment in 1922 of the firm of Atlee B. & Robert M. Ayres, Architects, and the adoption of the Spanish Colonial Revival style by Atlee as his favorite method of architectural expression. The superb residences for Thomas Hogg, Carl Newton, and Dr. Donald Atkinson captured the romantic image of the city's Spanish Colonial past. Robert M. Ayres, fresh from the architecture program at the University of Pennsylvania, was soon given major design responsibility, the most noted design being the octagonal Smith-Young Tower of 1929, which was to house the firm's offices on its 30th floor. Robert was also responsible for the design of the city's grandest private home, "Oak Court," for H. Lutcher Brown in 1935. The firm's range of work was enormous, encompassing such diverse products as the former Federal Reserve Bank and the spectacular Administration Building at Randolph Field.

GEORGE WILLIS, 1879-1960

RALPH CAMERON, 1892-1970

O'NEIL FORD, 1905-1982

Born in Chicago, George Willis arrived in San Antonio in 1910 with one of the best architectural educations obtainable at that time. He had studied at the Armour Institute, and from 1898 to 1902 was a member of Frank Lloyd Wright's studio, the latter training showing clearly in his early San Antonio commissions. The houses he designed for L. T. Wright at 342 Wilkins Avenue and Dr. Lemma Young at 828 Cambridge Oval are some of the finest Wrightian works in Texas. The Wright house, built in 1917, was Willis' first work upon leaving the office of Atlee B. Ayres. In the 1920s, Willis obtained other significant commissions, including the Milam Building and the San Antonio Country Club, the latter no longer standing. He was associated with Emmett T. Jackson on the design of the Builder's Exchange. Willis was also an associate along with Jackson and Atlee B. Ayres and Robert M. Ayres on the design of the San Antonio Municipal Auditorium of 1926. Willis maintained an office in the Smith-Young Tower until the time of his death in 1960, but his architectural output seems to have diminished significantly following the Second World War.

A native San Antonian, Ralph H. Cameron received at least part of his architectural training in Paris before he returned to San Antonio in 1912. He worked for the firm of Adams & Adams for two years before setting up his own practice. Within two years of opening his office, Cameron had achieved considerable success, serving as associate architect with Herbert Green on the design of the Scottish Rite Temple. Two years later Cameron received his most noted commission, that for the Medical Arts Building, now the Emily Morgan Hotel, famed for its ornate terra-cotta ornament in the Gothic style. He was also adept in residential design, as the delightful residence of F. E. Hornaday at 101 East Kings Highway clearly attests. Cameron was very active in the American Institute of Architects, and played a key role in the holding of the organization's 1932 National Convention in San Antonio. He was also a founding member of the Texas Society of Architects.

Otha Neil Ford personified the proverbial poor-boy-to-success story. From an humble birth in north-central Texas, he aspired to higher education and studied architecture by correspondence course. In 1926 he went to work for David R. Williams in Dallas, designing residences with a composite of regional characteristics. He and Williams drove hither and yon to supervise their work and observe historic Texas architecture *in situ*.

During the 1930s Williams helped Ford secure the 1939 federal commission for the La Villita restoration in San Antonio. In 1940 he settled with his wife Wanda at a stone house near San Jose Mission.

After wartime service, Ford resumed practice in San Antonio and began work on Trinity University with Bartlett Cocke and Harvey Smith in 1949. He designed a series of innovative facilities for the burgeoning Texas Instruments Company beginning in 1954. In the meantime he became a flamboyant lecturer on architecture and life, and achieved Fellowship in the AIA by 1960.

Ford formed a partnership with Boone Powell and Chris Carson in 1967, and together they designed numerous facilities at HemisFair '68. In the intervening years, the firm's work reflected Ford's penchant for regionally sensitive design. He died one year after the establishment of the O'Neil Ford Chair in Architecture at the University of Texas at Austin.

Building Index

Grants and Patrons

This guidebook was made possible in part by grants from:

TEXAS MASONRY INSTITUTE/SAN ANTONIO MASONRY INSTITUTE

H.E.B. COMPANY, SAN ANTONIO

Additional support was provided by the following San Antonio patrons:

Associated General Contractors/*San Antonio Chapter*

Robert Callaway

Chumney/Urrutia

Ford, Powell & Carson

Gerald D. Hines, Interests

JonesKell

Marmon Barclay Souter Foster Hays

MBank Alamo

Negley Paint Company

Redland Worth Corporation

Rehler Vaughn Beaty & Koone

San Antonio Conservation Society

Tobin Surveys